Trust Inc.

We are entering the age of sustainability – a business era where every company, big and small, must adapt its way of doing business to meet the realities of climate change, a finite supply of natural resources, evolving attitudes about inequality, increasing digitisation and automation. At the same time companies must meet the demands of consumers as they adjust to this rapidly changing way of life. Supercharging this change in consumer behaviour is social media – a communications revolution that is democratising and disrupting society in ways never seen before.

In this book, Matthew Yeomans explains why embracing sustainability is key to helping companies articulate their sense of purpose (and their reason to exist) in a world where social media is eroding trust in all institutions. The book shows how social media has made sustainability a mainstream concern for all society, how it compelled companies to be more authentic and accountable in their actions and how it will continue to shape how companies communicate the importance of sustainability to all of society.

This book is a powerful guide for both communication and marketing professionals in business, especially Fortune 500, FTSE 250 companies and agencies, on how to use social media to communicate with their audiences and stakeholders in an authentic way. It is also a guide/text book for the growing field of sustainability communication in higher education.

Matthew Yeomans is a writer, journalist and consultant with more than 25 years of experience working for, and advising, some of the world's largest publications and companies. He founded Sustainly, created the Social Media Sustainability Index and is the author of four books.

Trust Inc.

How Business Wins Respect in a Social Media Age

Matthew Yeomans

 Routledge
Taylor & Francis Group

LONDON AND NEW YORK

First published 2018
by Routledge
2 Park Square, Milton Park, Abingdon, Oxon OX14 4RN

and by Routledge
711 Third Avenue, New York, NY 10017

Routledge is an imprint of the Taylor & Francis Group, an informa business

© 2018 Matthew Yeomans

British Library Cataloguing-in-Publication Data
A catalogue record for this book is available from the British Library

Library of Congress Cataloging-in-Publication Data
A catalog record for this book has been requested

ISBN: 978-1-78353-810-2 (hbk)
ISBN: 978-1-78353-748-8 (pbk)
ISBN: 978-1-351-11163-8 (ebk)

Typeset in Garamond
by Apex CoVantage, LLC

Printed and bound by CPI Group (UK) Ltd, Croydon, CR0 4YY

Contents

Acknowledgements

This book has been taking shape in my head for the past four years but the roots of its reporting and my experience in the world of social media and sustainability go back more than a decade.

During that time a number of people have influenced my thinking and supported my work – especially this book. I'd like to thank my editor Rebecca Marsh for commissioning this work and for giving encouragement and advice when I found myself caught in two minds about what direction it should take. I'd also like to thank Judith Lorton for helping shepherd this manuscript into print.

A number of people have helped make this book possible. I'd like to thank the expert voices of Adam Elman, Michele Baeten, David Croft, Michael Dickstein, Teresa Herd, Dave Stangis and Alex Thompson who shared their sustainability knowledge and experiences with me in the form of Q&As for the book. I'd also like to thank Jamie Barnard and Virginie Helias for pointing me in the right direction when it came to interviews.

Thomas Kolster was a good friend and sounding board as I shaped the idea for the book and Tim Holmes was a much-needed critical reader of the manuscript and a kind host when I needed to escape to a secluded coastal retreat to write . . . as was my old friend Peter Kellam who similarly helped out.

Over the years I've learned a great deal about corporate sustainability by speaking at and attending Sustainable Brands conferences all around the world. I'd like to thank KoAnn Vikoren Skrzyniarz, Dimitar Vlahov, Sandra Pina and Jose Illana for inviting me to their events and making me a smarter person in the process.

This book couldn't have come about without the knowledge that I accrued running the Sustainly platform. And that wouldn't have been possible without the sterling editorial, research and design work of Andrew Weltch, Rachel England, Katee Hui, Anthony Kingsley, Sonia Malpeso and Andrew Roberts – all of whom have contributed to my knowledge of sustainability communication. Two other friends, Robert Leek and Neil Simmonds, were instrumental in helping Sustainly fly as was Martin McCabe, whose knowledge of virtual reality and digital creativity has greatly informed some of the thinking in this book. It also wouldn't have happened had I not gained the experience of running a social media consultancy and a business conference for nearly 10 years. My friends and former business partners from that time, Bernhard Warner and Mark Pigou, remain strong sources of support and continue to offer sage advice.

Finally, I'd like to thank my agent, Sharon Bowers, for her consistent support even in the face of my more half-baked ideas. And, most of all, I'd like to thank my wife (and all-important critical reader) Jowa and my kids Dylan and Zelda who have put up with me disappearing for weeks on end and countless chunks of weekends to get this book finished. Now I'm back . . . until the next book, of course.

Introduction

Which companies do you really care about? Is there one you simply couldn't do without?

It's a question that we rarely ask ourselves – so prevalent and dominant are companies and brands in our everyday lives. But while we're dependent on the products and services that enable our modern existence, do we really care who makes them?

Apple, many people will cry. Surely we can't live without Silicon Valley's minimalist yet superbly functional pads, pods and phones? Perhaps, but remember Apple had suffered over a decade of financial struggles before it dialled into global dominance with the iPhone. What about Coca-Cola then? Its signature product has helped establish perhaps the most iconic and best-loved brand the world has ever seen. But is Coca-Cola indispensable? As the world confronts its dangerous sugar addiction, perhaps not.

Pan Am, Amoco, Compaq, Polaroid, Circuit City, Blockbuster: the history of consumer culture is littered with once-dominant consumer brands that fell on hard times. Today, in the Internet age, the shelf life of major brands is shorter than ever before. Consider powerful brands like Facebook, Twitter and Instagram. None of these existed 15 years ago. Google is only 20 years old and Amazon just four years its senior. Yahoo and AOL, meanwhile, are mere shadows of their former greatness while once-promising social networks like MySpace, Friendster, Ning and Orkut have either died a complete digital death or exist in a moribund state – the lights may be on but no-one is using them.

The cut-throat nature of doing business in an online age where costs are slashed and profit margins squeezed by technological efficiencies, and where entire sectors can be disrupted by outsiders with the right algorithm, would be hard to navigate even in the most certain of times.

But this is anything but the most certain of times. Instead, our modern world currently faces a serious crisis of trust, or lack of.

That crisis of trust affects every part of society. Our collective faith in government and politics continues to be tested amid allegations of cyber manipulation of national and regional elections in the United States and Europe.

Our faith in the media is polarised along political lines to such a degree that politicians can seek to vilify media companies they don't like as "fake news". And, increasingly, the public's confidence in brands and corporations is eroding, partly as the more general suspicions of authority rub off on business but also because of a fundamental shift in the way that the public receives information and shapes their opinions.

As the 2017 Edelman Trust Barometer, a global survey of societal opinion, warned:

> With the fall of trust, the majority of respondents now lack full belief that the overall system is working for them. In this climate, people's societal and economic concerns, including globalization, the pace of innovation and eroding social values, turn into fears, spurring the rise of populist actions now playing out in several Western-style democracies.[1]

One of the biggest forces behind this shift and erosion of trust is social media – the communication revolution (now over a decade and a half old) that has given every person a voice, a community to connect and learn from, and, increasingly, a mini bully pulpit to hold companies, government and the media to account. Time and time again over the last 15 or so years social media–connected communities and platforms have challenged the hegemony of governments (as in the case of the Arab Spring), they have held law enforcement and the military to account on human rights failures (as the Black Lives Matters movement has shown) and they have called out companies and brands about faulty products, rotten or cynical customer services and arrogant governance.

Yet, even as social media has helped give people a clearer, more informed view of the world around them it has also been manipulated by some forces to confuse and distort people's sense of reality – not least in the political sphere. Our increasing reliance on the social media content shared by friends turbocharged the political information and opinion bubble we all naturally tend towards. With our ability to cherry pick the information we want to receive, and our tendency to share content only from friends with similar points of view as ours, the news we consume often does little but reinforce our established political worldview.

This polarisation of political discourse has been further stoked by new social media–only publishing operations – many of them promulgating blatantly false stories designed to be inflame the passions of readers so that they share them with their own "social media bubble". In many cases the motivation for these new political "news" sites is just to make money through advertising clicks and visits but, in some cases, social networks are being manipulated by governments to influence electorates both at home and abroad as the revelations about Russian interference in the 2016 US presidential election have made clear.

The social media–fuelled crisis of trust in business and society comes at a time when companies must also confront a series of migraine-inducing sustainability challenges that will affect how they do business in the future and influence society's trust in them.

Today's companies must plan for growing urbanisation and automation in society. They must secure access to raw materials, manage energy, and offer useful products in a world being defined by finite natural resources and where climate change is becoming an overarching business risk. They must maintain and nurture employees when a generation of young people are choosing to, or being forced to, look globally for work. And, as the world of transportation, banking and even health care is discovering, they must remain successful even as technologies like the Internet of Things, Cloud Computing and Blockchain allow new types of competitors to challenge and disrupt their business.

In many ways then, companies find themselves facing greater threats to the future of their business and to society than ever before at exactly the time when they need to regain the trust of a new type of connected and informed consumer.

How then can companies win back the trust of the public and society? The answer, this book will argue, is through embracing and integrating sustainability throughout business while demonstrating that commitment through communication.

Most in the world of marketing, advertising, public relations and customer service already understand the crisis of trust that threatens to engulf business. There's a reason why authenticity, transparency and community have become the corporate buzzwords of the social media age. But in today's always-on, smarter-than-before society, pledging to be a better company just won't cut it. You have to demonstrate how your company is creating a better experience for consumers and, yes, society.

Just a few years ago most corporate communicators and marketers would have dismissed the notion that consumers care about sustainability. They would cite studies that showed "ethical" consumers made up just a small portion of total sales, and that mainstream shoppers wouldn't pay a premium for "green" products. Surely it was obvious that the public didn't care about sustainable sourcing and supply chains, never mind ethical working practices? These were the sort of dull achievements best left for corporate communication channels.

But isn't the price we pay for products a question of sustainability? Consider, for example, the cost of growing the crops and raising the livestock to supply the food we consume. How can farmers and food workers make a living when the prices in the supermarkets are so cheap? What about the reliance on ingredients like corn sugar and salt to boost the taste of low-cost food? Are these foods sustaining us or making us ill? The same core questions can be asked of the detergents and soap we use, the clothes we buy, the cars we drive and the services we depend on to run our modern life.

These are all sustainability questions that consumers ask every day online and offline, and which affect their purchasing decisions. What's more, many consumers either work for major companies or have families and friends who do. So working conditions, tolerance of diversity, and gender equality also have particular resonance and influence their opinion of companies and brands.

The actions of concerned (and connected consumers) already are having an impact. They are prompting fast-food companies to change their menus. They are forcing food producers to take a stand on genetically modified crops and retailers to shift to organic supply chains. They are pushing household and personal goods manufacturers to use non-toxic components in cleaning products. They are holding apparel makers to account over working conditions in their factories and those of their suppliers. And they are putting pressure on the world of business to enforce tolerance of people and to offer the equal opportunities to succeed. All of these issues sit at the heart of sustainability in business and influence people's buying decisions. It's just when real people talk about them they don't use the language of corporate sustainability.

It's not just consumers and communicators that have this disconnect. Within companies themselves, the language used by sustainability professionals can leave the marketing and communication departments scratching their heads and struggling for a way to communicate sustainability to the outside world.

This book is made up of three parts. The first, "The social age," documents the growth of social media and its disruptive impact on the world of business; how online environmental activism helped make sustainability a mainstream concern within business; and how companies learned the hard way that they had to listen to, not shout at, social media communities.

The second part, "The trust factors," explores how companies are trying to regain the trust of the public through collaboration with social media communities; radical transparency about how they operate; providing leadership on sustainability issues; empowering and educating; and inspiring consumer behaviour change.

The final part of the book, "The know how," examines how companies have successfully communicated the sustainability work they do so that it builds trust with the public; how companies embrace and expand sustainability reporting to help power storytelling; and, finally, how the United Nations Sustainable Development Goals can provide a blueprint for regaining the trust of society and building a sustainable future for companies.

A personal note

This book has grown out of 15 years' personal experience writing about and providing consulting services on the impact of social media and sustainability on society. My career began as a journalist in New York in the late 1980s working for the *Village Voice* newspaper. By the late early 2000s I was covering both environmental issues and technology for a number of publications including *The Industry Standard*, *Salon* and *Wired*. Through my writing and editing work I came to appreciate the many ways the Internet and World Wide Web were starting to reshape our world – breaking down the barriers to information that existed in the past while radically changing the way we consumed media in all its forms.

The explosion in blogging and new social media platforms came just as I was transitioning away from full-time journalism into university lecturing and providing online communication consulting services to companies. By early 2006 I'd earned the dubious accolade of being a "social media expert" – mainly because I'd co-founded the United Kingdom's first conference devoted to social media in business, appropriately named Blogging4Business.

In reality I was hardly an expert, but I did understand how content and publishing worked – social media was, at its heart, a publishing medium. Soon, with my friend, business partner and fellow journalist Bernhard Warner, I was advising the likes of Lloyds Banking Group and HSBC on social media reputation issues while charting new social media trends for publications like Slate's *The Big Money*. We even entered the world of advertising at one point, having been recruited to launch a new social media agency in London.

It didn't last long. For one thing our approach to social media storytelling proved an uneasy fit with an advertising sector still dominated by an old-school approach to persuading the public. But for me the misfit ran deeper than simply communication planning. What had fascinated me about social media from the start was its potential to help companies foster more authentic relationships with their customers, yet many of the marketing clients I dealt with saw social media as just another way of selling stuff or creating buzz.

Surely social media could offer more for companies? That was the question that started me on a seven-year exploration of the ways social media was providing a platform for sustainability. In late 2010 I published a new piece of research, *The Social Media Sustainability Index*, that studied the way Fortune 500 and FTSE 100 companies were communicating their sustainability work using social media. Over the years this piece of research grew so that by 2016 I was analysing the sustainability communication strategies of more than 450 global companies.

Out that research, the writing that sprung from it, and the consulting with brands and companies that was informed by it, comes this book. It is, as you can see, in some ways the story of my last 15 years. I hope you find useful what I've lived through and learned from during that time.

Note

1 https://www.edelman.com/trust2017/

Part 1

The social age

Chapter 1

A short history of social media

Breaking the lock on corporate message control

On the evening of September 12, 2004, a 25-year old cycling enthusiast called Chris Brennan posted a detailed description on Bikeforums.net of how he had "cracked" the supposedly unbreakable Kryptonite Evolution 2000 bike lock with nothing more than a disposable ball-point pen. Using the alias – you could say pen name – *Unaesthetic* – Brennan titled his post: "Your Brand New Bicycle U-Lock Is not Safe!" Little could he have imagined the shock his actions would send through the corporate world.[1]

Brennan's revelation wasn't exactly new – there had long been plenty of chat in biking circles about the vulnerability of u-locks. Back in 1992 the BBC had written about it but the story failed to get any traction.

What made Brennan's post so damaging (and so profound in the short but very busy history of social media) was his audience. Within days, bloggers and message board posters were sharing news of the lock hack. One prominent voice was a new tech blog, Engadget. To amplify its message, it created a short video showing readers exactly how to use a ball-point pen to break the lock.

Engadget's post went "viral," to use the language of the nascent blogosphere. Attuned to this new social media chatter, *The New York Times* published its own story about Kryptonite's product weakness.[2] In a piece titled "The Pen Is Mightier than the Lock" the newspaper noted how nearly 170,000 people had seen Brennan's posting in a just a few days, "starting a full-fledged panic".

By the time millions of other readers had finished reading *The New York Times* story – including senior executives at Kryptonite – the company knew it had a major problem on its hands. Either it could claim the Engadget video was fake or it could admit its lock wasn't as secure as the company claimed.

Ultimately Kryptonite would recall locks en masse, costing the company some $10 million. In the process "a 50-year-old lock design was rendered useless" was how *Wired* magazine summed up Kryptonite's predicament[3] – all because one newspaper reporter and one new tech blogger were reading one bike enthusiast's online message board.

Other companies hoping that Kryptonite's problems couldn't happen to them were soon disappointed as bloggers began to grasp the new consumer clout they possessed when complaining about faulty products and bad customer service.

Just a few months later, on June 21, 2005, Jeff Jarvis, a media journalist and one of the leading lights of the early blogging movement posted this tirade: "Dell lies. Dell sucks. I just got a new Dell laptop and paid a fortune for the four-year, in home service. The machine is a lemon and the service is a lie." Over the next three days, Jarvis posted on his blog about the hair-tearing experience of dealing with nearly non-existent Dell customer service to try and get his laptop fixed.

As Jarvis complained about his experience first on his blog and then in his weekly *Guardian* media column, other Dell customers left comments expressing similar frustration with the company. By giving voice to his "Dell Hell" (as Jarvis titled one of his blog posts) he not only exposed the lack of trust many customers felt towards the company but he also became a mainstream and high-profile torchbearer for what media commentators were starting to term "social media" – a democratising online movement where anybody writing a blog had the power to publish their thoughts and opinions, share what they read on other blogs and in the media and to directly connect and network with other bloggers.

As Jarvis vented: "We are in the new era of 'Seller beware.' Now, when you screw your customers, your customers can fight back and publish and organize."[4]

(To make matters worse for Dell, in mid-2006, another new tech blog, Gizmodo, published video footage of a Dell laptop exploding at a conference in Japan. The laptop was powered by a Sony battery and commenters were quick to add their own personal experiences of other Sony battery blow-ups.)

Looking back now, in a social media age where Facebook, Twitter, Instagram, Snapchat and YouTube dominate our daily lives so much, it hardly seems possible that, little more than a decade ago, most people didn't have their own social media voice to hold companies to account. Today all brands and most companies understand they need some presence in social media and that, by doing so, they agree to have a two-way conversation with the public. Platforms like Pinterest and Instagram operate as virtual shop windows for many consumer brands; Facebook offers millions of fans who are amenable to conversational marketing; while, for many consumer-facing companies, Twitter operates as a de facto customer service channel.

But in 2006, the experiences of Kryptonite, Sony and Dell sent shock waves through public relations, corporate communication, marketing and customer service departments – and for one key reason. Over the previous 100 years nearly every major company and brand had sacrificed having an honest and authentic relationship with the people who bought its products in the pursuit of more sales and higher profits.

How advertising created a corporate monster

The communication and creative industries powered the growth of modern corporations through the success of mass marketing.

The first breakthrough in brand advertising came in mid 19th century Paris when a painter, Jules Cheret, transformed the long-established tradition of creating posters to advertise services by producing colour versions featuring attractive half-clothed women.[5]

The powers of persuasion soon took a darker, more cynical turn in the United States through the sales and marketing of patent medicines – particularly through the work of one man, a former preacher called Claude Hopkins. In the early years of the 20th century he was at the forefront of an early "wellness" industry that conjured fake claims of miracle cures to exploit the health fears of the populace. Hopkins' genius was to turn the local exploits of travelling "snake oil" salesmen into a national business by taking inspiration from the successful mail-order catalogues run by Sears and Montgomery Ward.

Both companies used the federally subsidised US Post Office to market their catalogues. Hopkins did the same – sending out more than 400,000 pamphlets advertising nerve tonics for Dr. Shoop's Restorative. Buoyed by the success of this target marketing, Hopkins next applied his newly honed direct-mail techniques to convince American households that another useless product, Liquozone, could relieve ailments including malaria, anthrax and even cancer.

After a series of newspaper investigations into the dubious claims of the patent medicine industry, the US Congress clamped down on this hucksterism with new regulations requiring "truth in labelling" to avoid misbranding or false claims of cure-alls.

The new regulation prompted the rapid decline of the patent medicine industry, but Hopkins would soon find a new vocation for his hoodwinking skills – marketing products like cigarettes, orange juice and toothpaste as a guru for Chicago's Lord & Thomas advertising agency.[6]

As Tim Wu writes in his history of media manipulation, *The Attention Merchants*:

> It is easy to ascribe the success of such hokum to the gullibility of another age, until we stop to reflect that the techniques successfully used to sell patent medicine are still routinely used today. The lotions and potions of our times inevitably promise youthfulness, health, or weight loss, thanks to exotic ingredients like antioxidants, amino acids, miracle fruits like the pomegranate and acai berry, extracted ketones, or biofactors.[7]

And he makes clear the smoke and mirrors isn't restricted just to health and beauty.

> As devotees of technology we are, if anything, more susceptible to the supposed degree of difference afforded by some ingenious proprietary

innovation, like the "air" in Nike's sports shoes, triple reverse osmosis in some brands of water, or the gold-plating of audio components.[8]

The arrival of mass production – kickstarted in no small part by Henry Ford's 1908 Model T – presented many new opportunities for advertising to demonstrate how it could shape the desires of the public, even if Ford insisted, "If you really have a good thing, it will advertise itself."[9]

The Model T gave hundreds of thousands of Americans their first taste of driving but it also changed the United States' sense of itself – creating a more outward, modern and materialistic view of life that the marketing world was all too happy to appeal to. The monochrome conformity of the Model T might have worked for the first ever mass-market automobile but not for the second generation of vehicles and car owners.

Having learned from the highly effective propaganda techniques employed by governments in the World War One, advertising and public relations agencies now started manufacturing consent on a mass scale. Agencies like J. Walter Thompson, McCann Erickson, WS Crawford and BBDO transformed what had been a regional ad hoc approach to advertising in a national and, later, international mass attention industry. Marketing campaigns for the new brands being created were unrelenting and advertising in the post-war years became ubiquitous. The advertising industry was also helping reshape the economy. "In the United States the average household went from spending a mere $79 per year on durable goods at the turn of the century to $279 by the 1920s," Wu notes.[10]

Products were marketed based on their scientific validation, their luxury connotations, their ability to cure new health issues (sound familiar?) and also their appeal to either men or women separately. To further hook consumers into the repeat purchases necessary to maintain the new mass production economy, companies invested heavily in creating new brands that the advertising could then manufacture demand for.

Increased prosperity as the United States and European economies recovered from the World War Two gave consumerism a fresh impetus and advertising took full advantage of the new mass media of radio and then television to stoke material desires.

Cars were marketed based on their colours, the allure of whitewall wheels, and additional features like radios, sunroofs and cruise control that demonstrated extra degrees of affluence and consumer know-how. Eating out at new fast-food restaurants like McDonald's became a visible yet affordable demonstration of post-war posterity. Even a mineral that, at the turn of the 20th century, no-one really knew about would be transformed into the ultimate object of desire thanks to a 1947 advertising campaign: "A Diamond Is Forever."[11]

By the early 21st century, then, the corporate world had created a completely dominant mass-market culture engineered to devour the volume of products and services it was producing – all fed by the advertising, marketing and public relations industry. Customers became consumers in the minds of brands. And with millions of them to "reach," brands had to become experts at creating advertising and public relations campaigns that talked *at* consumers rather than *with* them.

The advent of online marketing further exacerbated this disconnect by creating an industry where every digital interaction with an advert or marketing message could, in theory, be measured. By 2006 marketing and online business in general had become very much a numbers game – judged by digital impressions and click-throughs, open rates on direct email campaigns and increasingly tortuous rationalisations about what return on marketing investment actually looked like.

Drunk on data, companies thought they were getting better insight on consumer behaviour than ever before. What they failed to realise was that data means little if you don't understand the motivations and feelings of the people buying or not buying your products. If companies had been less fixated on the numbers they might have spotted that, thanks to new technologies, consumers were starting to find their voice and that the balance of power in the brand–consumer dynamic was changing. After all, the first signs of the social media revolution had been apparent for a long time.

The roots of a connected society

In 2000, four smart Bay Area digital voices, David Weinberger, Doc Searls, Rick Levine and Christopher Locke, published a piece of business thinking, *The Cluetrain Manifesto*, that offered a damning and insightful indictment of the dysfunctional relationship between brands and the public.[12] The manifesto offered a blueprint for rebuilding that relationship based around human interaction and transparent, authentic communication, and it was anchored by a series of statements of which these five encapsulated the communication revolution taking hold:

- "Markets are conversations. Markets consist of human beings, not demographic sectors."
- "The Internet is enabling conversations among human beings that were simply not possible in the era of mass media."
- "These networked conversations are enabling powerful new forms of social organization and knowledge exchange to emerge."
- "Companies that assume online markets are the same markets that used to watch their ads on television are kidding themselves."
- "Companies can now communicate with their markets directly. If they blow it, it could be their last chance."[13]

The Cluetrain Manifesto would become the bible for those in business who came to see social media not just as a philosophy for authentic communication but as an agent to rescue the corporate world from its own arrogance and excess. It grew out of a widely held frustration at the end of the 20th century that the initial egalitarian promise of the Internet and the World Wide Web had become subverted and co-opted by the mass-market machinery of big business.

The manifesto drew its inspiration from an earlier generation of subversive techies – the real forerunners of the social media – who, starting in the late 1970s, pioneered using the Internet for community conversation and collaboration through Bulletin Board Systems (BBS).

In relatively simple terms, the way BBS culture worked was that, by using a dial-up modem – short for modulator-demodulator – digital information could be modulated into an analogue signal that then could be transmitted through phone lines. At the other end of the phone connection the receiver's modem took the carrier signal and demodulated it into digital information that could be processed through a computer.[14]

Modems had been in existence since World War Two, but the growth of personal computing in the 1980s brought the potential of this connectivity to hundreds of thousands of new PC users. In 1978, snowed in during a blizzard, two Chicago-based computer enthusiasts, Ward Christensen and Randy Suess, set about establishing an online connection and location for Chicago computer geeks to congregate. The fruits of their labour was the Computerized Bulletin Board System – the first ever BBS.

As *The Atlantic Monthly* wrote in an article titled "The Lost Civilization of Dial Up Bulletin Boards":

> BBSes once numbered in the tens of thousands in North America. These mostly text-based, hobbyist-run services played a huge part in the online landscape of the 1980s and '90s. Anyone with a modem and a home computer could dial-in, often for free, and interact with other callers in their area code.[15]

In 1985 Stewart Brand, founder of the counter-culture bible, *Whole Earth Catalog*, launched a BBS in San Francisco called Whole Earth 'Lectronic Link (or WELL for short) with Larry Brilliant (who would later go on to run Google's philanthropic arm). In 1990 Stacey Horn started a New York equivalent, EchoNYC, devoted to media, film, literature and sexual culture in the city. What was notable about both these BBSes was that they enabled online community interaction and collaboration around a range of topics – not just computer geek chat.[16] Users of these systems were sowing the seeds of social media.

While the topics of conversation were quite broad, you still had to be a little geeky to use a BBS – it's no surprise that future digital icons like John Perry Barlow (founder of the Electronic Frontier Foundation), Craig Newmark (founder of Craigslist) and Steve Case (founder of AOL) all frequented

The WELL. Other mainstream dial-up communities like AOL and CompuServe helped bring more people online, but it was the invention of the World Wide Web by Tim Berners Lee in 1989 and the subsequent release of web browsers like Netscape in 1994 and Internet Explorer in 1995 that sped up online democratisation by offering an easy way to navigate the thousands of new online sites that were being created.

The early web pioneers envisaged a utopian environment of free expression, knowledge sharing and creativity. Within a few years, though, it was clear that the web would be dominated by the same forces of business that had so quickly embraced radio and TV in the decades before.

The web and its potential audience of millions became a go-to destination for media companies and newspapers seeking to grow their audience. In 1994 the *Daily Telegraph* launched the United Kingdom's first news website. One year later, former San Francisco *Examiner* editor, David Talbot, launched *Salon* – an online-only news site. *The New York Times* started its own website in 1996.[17] The growth of online news required funding, of course. While companies like the *Wall Street Journal* introduced a subscription model, most other newspapers decided that digital advertising was the best way to make money on the web. Media companies weren't alone in identifying the Internet's potential: an entire new breed of company now started to emerge – one that eschewed the need for physical stores and, instead, sold directly to consumers online.

The growth of dot-coms like Amazon, eBay, Alibaba and others were evidence that the corporate world had stolen the web's soul in the eyes of Internet purists. That was true in as much as e-commerce now became the driving force of online growth. Yet these feisty Internet start-ups brought with them an outsider mentality that not only challenged the traditional power of bricks-and-mortar companies but also introduced a culture of online accountability that most businesses had never had to deal with.

Central to this culture was the power to comment on products and services through reviews or online feedback. Now e-commerce companies had to be open and prepared to have a conversation with the people they wanted to sell to – a conversation that would increase exponentially as new technologies introduced a revolution in online personal publishing.

In 1997, the first weblog was published (soon to be shortened in online slang to "blog") and in 1999 the first blogging platform, LiveJournal, launched offering anyone free access to online publishing even if they had no prior coding experience. It was soon joined by other free hosted blogging platforms including Blogger and Typepad as well as Movable Type and WordPress, both of which offered blogging templates that could be hosted on a personal website.

The power to publish online without having to design and build a website was a real breakthrough for personal publishing, but what really gave the blogging movement power was the community that built up around it.

A key functionality of these new blogs was the ease of adding hyperlinks to specific content on other blogs and websites. Not only did this allow bloggers to highlight conversations from other bloggers that interested them, but they could also use the links to create a "Blogroll" of their favourite blogs – a form of validation that increased the sense of community and drove web traffic to their sites. This in turn created a digital pecking order that saw some really popular bloggers rise to so-called A-List status.

The influence of the blogging community and its powers of collaboration became clear in 2004 when the veteran TV news anchor, Dan Rather, had his career derailed by a group of conservative political bloggers. Working together in real time, they picked holes in and discredited the reporting of a Rather-fronted CBS programme that questioned President George W. Bush's Air National Guard service during the Vietnam War. Looking back now at the speed which the political sleuthing work of these blogs, led by Little Green Footballs,[18] spread through the conservative blogosphere, it's clear that the political bubble effect existed even in the earliest days of social media.[19]

Another power shift that blogging brought about (and would be exacerbated by the explosion of social media) was the power to choose what content people wanted to read online. For centuries, the world's media diet had been dictated first by the pamphleteers, then newspapers, magazines, radio programs and television stations. Despite the growth of cable television starting in the 1980s, and the cult following for underground zines, most people's choice of media content in the early 2000s was still limited to what professional media publishers had to offer. Blogs radically altered that dynamic as thousands of new voices sprang up offering news, ideas and opinions on hobbies, topics and current events. Now, if you cared deeply about trout fishing, vegan cooking or even something as random as the inner workings of washing machines[20] you were no longer restricted to the ramblings of Angler's Mail, The Vegan Society or the Whitegoods Trade Association. Instead, with a quick search of the blogosphere using a nascent social media search tool like Technorati you could find like-minded blogs and connect with them.

The network effect

Six Degrees, founded back in 1997, is generally credited as the first social networking site, though it was Friendster, launched in 2002, that made mainstream the concept of having one online community to connect and stay updated with friends and meet new people through similar interests or connections.

Within months Friendster faced competition from new networks. LinkedIn launched in 2003 and was dedicated to professional connections. Next came hi5, which attracted users from Asia and South America. MySpace, with its focus on music, launched the same year, while early in 2004 Google – by now the world's biggest online company – decided to dip its toes into the world of social networking with its Orkut platform. Then, in February 2004, Mark Zuckerberg unleashed The Facebook on the Harvard University campus – though the college-focused network, by then stripped of its awkward preposition, wouldn't be available to the general public until 2006.

That same year, another new social network called Twitter was causing a major stir among the media and the thousands of digerati attendees at that year's South By Southwest conference. Founded in San Francisco in 2006[21] by Jack Dorsey, Noah Glass, Biz Stone and Ev Williams (the latter had earlier created Blogger and would later found the Medium platform) Twitter began life with very different intentions to Facebook. In fact, while Zuckerburg's network very quickly grasped the commercial appeal and power of marrying its users with brands, Twitter struggled to define exactly what it stood for or how it could convert its platform into a profitable and sustainable business (a flaw that continues to this day).[22]

But while Twitter might have been lacked strategic direction, it soon established itself as one of the most influential social media platforms due to its ability to harness and organise mass dialogue around a topic or news event. Twitter's main tool for collaborating ideas and opinions was the hashtag – first introduced in 2007 by user Chris Messina who, in a tweet, suggested "using # (pound) for groups" to help organise conversations.[23]

Hashtags weren't an immediate success. Twitter's functionality was already considered a somewhat geeky form of communicating compared with the more user-friendly experience offered by Facebook. As Messina wrote on his own blog in 2007, "People are either lukewarm to them or are annoyed and hate them. I get it. I do. But for some stupid reason I just can't leave them alone."[24]

But it was the speed at which information was shared over Twitter that drove interest and participation, and this viral quality made the network a perfect vehicle for following breaking news and crises.

One such crisis – wildfires around San Diego in the summer of 2007 – drove the mainstream adoption of hashtags. A friend of Messina's posted reports of how the wildfires were spreading using the hashtag #sandiegofire and other Twitter users followed suit. News and information (not all of it from official news sources, of course) was now trackable through Twitter.

As Messina wrote: "Hashtags become even more useful in a time of crisis or emergency as groups can rally around a common term to facilitate tracking, as demonstrated today with the San Diego fires."

Little could Messina have known that his invention would soon help organise and shape the rallying cry for global political protests (as happened during the Iran elections in 2009 and the Arab Spring uprising in 2011[25]) and consumer campaigns run both by brands for marketing purposes and against them in protest at substandard products, services and corporate behaviour.

A social media power shift

If the corporate world had been paying more attention to what its customers felt about it rather than simply trying to sell them more "stuff," it would have identified a growing crisis of confidence in the way companies and brands were conducting themselves.

Part of the concern came from a growing realisation on the part of the public that companies didn't really care that much about real people apart from trying to sell them more products. The early days of brand social media interactions on Twitter and Facebook were often marked by anger and exasperated cries for help by customers who had discovered a direct channel of contact after years of being managed by public relations or rebuffed by customer service.

Faced with a consumer backlash, some companies realised the need to "engage" with consumers (to use the business jargon of the time) using social networks and online forums. Dell, stung by its Hell experience, was one of the first companies to engage directly with its customers using a blog and a dedicated social customer feedback platform. Dell IdeaStorm (based on an idea that Salesforce CEO Mark Benioff shared with Dell's founder Michael Dell)[26] launched in 2007 offering consumers not just advice on their hardware problems but also a platform where they could suggest ways for Dell to improve its products and service.

Starbucks further developed this concept of collaborative feedback with My Starbucks Idea, another Salesforce platform aimed at developing a sense of community but also making sure that any overt criticism of the brand stayed in an internal safe space where Starbucks could manage and respond quickly.

Tapping into this brand angst, a number of new technology companies launched offering social media monitoring services to listen and analyse consumer chat.

The names of these new companies – Brandwatch, Buzzmetrics, Market Sentinel, Social Mention – reflected how social media represented both a major threat to companies' reputation and also a huge opportunity for marketing and selling to consumers.

During the period 2005 to 2009 hundreds of other social media analytics start-ups joined the fray, mining social media conversational data, accompanied by a small army of consultants and public relations firms looking to glean gold nuggets of insight from the sometimes enlightening but often inane ramblings of a general populace intoxicated with its power to share its opinions online.

By early 2009 Facebook boasted 350 million members and had established itself as the world's biggest social network at the expense of MySpace.[27] This number would nearly double in 2010 and, as the platform went global and mainstream, so its influence in terms of brand marketing and reputation also grew.

Companies and brands rushed to create their own dedicated Facebook pages (or as in the case of Coca-Cola they acquired pages that had been set up by fans[28]) and to create branded YouTube and Twitter channels. At the same time the advertising and public relations world scrambled to create new agencies and services that could help companies navigate the social media world.[29]

By the end of the 21st century's first decade social media marketing and advertising along with the growing area of online conversation analytics was a multi-billion-dollar business. But despite all the resources being channelled to target social network users most companies and brands still didn't fully appreciate the extent to which a new generation of connected consumers would force them to adopt a more responsible approach to business and to greater society.

Notes

1 www.bikeforums.net/general-cycling-discussion/67493-your-brand-new-bicycle-u-lock-not-safe.html
2 www.nytimes.com/2004/09/17/nyregion/the-pen-is-mightier-than-the-lock.html
3 www.wired.com/2004/09/twist-a-pen-open-a-lock/
4 Charlene Li and Josh Bernoff (2011). *Groundswell*. Harvard Business Press, p. 206.
5 Tim Wu (2017), *The Attention Merchants*. Atlantic Books, p. 18.
6 Wu, *The Attention Merchants*, p. 52.
7 Tim Wu: *The Attention Merchants* p. 54.
8 Wu, *The Attention Merchants* p. 30.
9 www.thehenryford.org/explore/blog/advertising-the-model-t/
10 Wu, *The Attention Merchants*, p. 53.
11 www.theatlantic.com/international/archive/2015/02/how-an-ad-campaign-invented-the-diamond-engagement-ring/385376/
12 www.cluetrain.com/
13 *The Cluetrain Manifesto*. Preface, page XXII.
14 http://ethw.org/Bulletin_Board_Systems
15 www.theatlantic.com/technology/archive/2016/11/the-lost-civilization-of-dial-up-bulletin-board-systems/506465/
16 www.theatlantic.com/technology/archive/2012/07/what-the-wells-rise-and-fall-tell-us-about-online-community/259504/
17 In the summer of 1996 I created the first online presence for *The Village Voice*. It was a website devoted to the Presidential Election national conventions in San Diego and Chicago. It was called Convention Confidential.
18 http://littlegreenfootballs.com/article/12526_Bush_Guard_Documents-_Forged
19 It's also worth pointing out that Dan Rather would later regain his journalistic voice and find a new audience through social media.
20 Yes, in 2008 there really was a YouTube channel devoted to measuring the sound and speed of washing machine spin cycles.
21 www.lifewire.com/history-of-twitter-3288854
22 www.bloomberg.com/gadfly/articles/2017-07-27/twitter-is-still-sad-and-a-turnaround-is-questionable
23 https://gigaom.com/2010/04/30/the-short-and-illustrious-history-of-twitter-hashtags/
24 https://factoryjoe.com/2007/10/22/twitter-hashtags-for-emergency-coordination-and-disaster-relief/

25 www.theglobeandmail.com/news/world/year-in-hashtags-tweets-from-the-arab-spring/article641751/
26 Li and Bernoff, *Groundswell*, p. 210.
27 www.the*Guardian*.com/news/datablog/2014/feb/04/facebook-in-numbers-statistics
28 http://adage.com/article/digital/coke-fans-brought-brand-facebook-fame/135238/
29 In 2008 I became part of this frenzy when I was recruited by Omnicom to co-launch a new social media agency in London.

Chapter 2

How social media made sustainability mainstream

Upton Sinclair's 1906 novel, *The Jungle,* is often credited as the first landmark media exposure of corporate malfeasance. It told the story of a young Lithuanian couple, Jurgis Rudkus and Ona Lukoszaite, who move to Chicago at the turn of the 20th century where Jurgis goes to work in Packingtown, the heart of the city's meatpacking industry.[1] Sinclair, a journalist, spent weeks researching and reporting the story that he would ultimately turn into prose. What he discovered was shocking both in terms of the conditions that immigrants were forced to work under and the food safety standards (or lack of) that the industry adhered to.

"This is no fairy story and no joke," Sinclair wrote. "The meat will be shovelled into carts and the man who did the shovelling will not trouble to lift out a rat even when he saw one." That was the least of the food contamination. At times workers fell into the machinery and became part of the food chain.

The Jungle was an instant hit – it sold 5,000 copies on the first day of publication and caused outrage among the US public over meat standards. Ultimately it would prove highly influential in shaping new regulations on working conditions and food safety in the fast-industrialising United States.[2]

Sinclair's work kicked off a new era of hard-hitting investigative journalism – "muckraking" as it became known – that focused on corporate excess and the dereliction of social and environmental duty. Just five years after *The Jungle* was published, harrowing newspaper coverage of the Triangle Shirtwaist Fire in New York City where 146 workers died – most of them young women and many of them locked in the building – helped herald in new working and safety condition laws for garment workers.

In 1920 the *Boston Post* blew the lid on the activities of the Security Exchange Company, led by one Charles Ponzi whose name would forever afterwards be associated with fraudulent investment schemes. Five years later *The New York Times* exposed safety shortcomings at a Standard Oil refinery in Bayway, New Jersey that resulted in workers falling sick from exposure to tetraethyl lead – referred to at the time as "looney gas".[3] And in 1935 a publication called *New Masses* published an expose of how 2,000 construction workers at Union

Carbide's Hawk's Nest Tunnel project in West Virginia became afflicted by a deadly respiratory disease after breathing silica.

World War Two shifted the priorities of both media and society alike. Companies and workers became part of the collective war effort and – with a common set of enemies in the form of Germany, Italy and Japan – few major publications in the United States or the United Kingdom had the editorial appetite to dig too deeply into the workings of the corporate world.

By the time the 1950s arrived, following a decade of war and austerity, a newly optimistic consumer class was too enamoured with being able to own a new car, washing machine and even a TV to worry too much about how these products were made or the damage that was caused in their production.

It wasn't until the 1962 publication of *Silent Spring*, Rachel Carson's three-part *New Yorker* investigation into the effects of the pesticide DDT on the environment (and bird populations in particular), that the public started to question whether the corporate world was acting in their best interests. Carson's reporting, later published in a best-selling book, made clear that environmental damage being caused by pesticides was no accident. Instead Carson accused the chemical industry in the United States of spreading disinformation and government officials of being complicit in the lies.

Silent Spring arrived at a time when the word of corporations – especially around claims of scientific breakthroughs and know-how – was pretty much still taken for granted. The outrage around its discoveries punctured the idea that companies could or should be trusted and is widely credited as the catalyst for the modern environmental movement which, by extension, exerted the political pressure that drove the formation of the US Environmental Protection Agency (EPA) in 1970.[4]

Carson's critique of corporate America was reinforced by consumer activist Ralph Nader in his 1965 dissection of the automobile industry, *Unsafe at Any Speed*. The book claimed that carmakers had resisted introducing seat belts and were reluctant to spend money on improving driver and passenger safety. It was particularly damning of one vehicle – the Chevrolet Corvair. What Carson had done in terms of raising concerns about corporate environmental misdeeds, Nader, along with other agitating voices like journalist James Ridgeway,[5] brought to consumer product safety.

Corporate bad guys from central casting

Public suspicion of corporations only increased in the 1970s – a decade that saw the birth of Earth Day and a growing awareness of the fragility of the planet, the effects of pollution and the outsized influence that corporations were playing in everyday lives.

Echoing Nader's concerns a decade before, US consumers and the media began to get suspicious of the high number of gas tank explosions suffered by Ford Pinto drivers when they were hit from behind. Lawsuits and subsequent court depositions would reveal that Ford had been aware of the fire risk since the car first went into production back in 1970. Most damaging to the company, though, were memos published by writer Mark Dowie in *Mother Jones* magazine that showed Ford had undertaken a detailed cost analysis of its corporate liability should it have to compensate crash victims.[6]

Food and nutrition also became an issue for the public in the 1970s. As the food journalist, Michael Pollan, wrote in a *New York Review of Books* essay in 2010:

> Until the early 1970s, when a bout of food price inflation and the appearance of books critical of industrial agriculture (by Wendell Berry, Francis Moore Lappé, and Barry Commoner, among others) threatened to propel the subject to the top of the national agenda, Americans ha[d] not had to think very hard about where their food comes from, or what it is doing to the planet, their bodies, and their society.[7]

Soon, a litany of food scandals were causing the public in the United States and Europe to ask serious questions about what they were eating. As described in *Eating Traditional Food*:

> More environmental and unsafe food scandals followed [the publication of *Silent Spring*]: mercury in freshwater fish, arsenic in chicken meat, hormones in beef, salmonella in canned soup. . . . These scandals deeply impressed the public in the US and caused strong reaction in Western Europe.[8]

At the time the corporate bete noir for environmental and social activists undoubtedly was Nestlé. In 1974 the UK non-governmental organisation (NGO), War on Want, published *The Baby Killer,* a damning report that accused multinational baby food producers (and Nestlé in particular) of causing infant illness and death in poor communities by promoting bottle feeding and discouraging breastfeeding. So effective was the multinational marketing campaigns in some emerging markets that many mothers, unable to afford enough of the formula, started mixing it with too much water, causing infant malnutrition and stunted development.[9]

Writing in the *Guardian* in 2013, the original author of the *War on Want* report, Mike Muller, explained how Nestlé sued Swiss activists for titling their version of the report *Nestlé Kills Babies* and won the libel case.

However, the judge warned Nestlé that if the company did not want to face accusations of causing death and illness through sales practices such as using sales reps dressed in nurses' uniforms, it should change the way that it did business.

That shocked the company by undercutting the socially committed self-image that Nestlé had been projecting ever since its founding in 1905. The

War on Want report also "launched a long-running global campaign [that is still cited today], proving that networked social action was possible even in snail mail days,"[10] Muller wrote.

A decade marked by defeat in Vietnam, the fall of President Richard Nixon, an oil and energy crisis sparked by OPEC, and the Iran hostage crisis all contributed to a growing sense of insecurity in America and an erosion of trust in government and corporate institutions. These fears were reflected not just in newspaper coverage and advertising (the iconic Keep America Beautiful environmental advert featuring "Crying Indian" Iron Eyes Cody aired on Earth Day in 1971[11]) but also through the powerful medium of film.

All the President's Men, released in 1976, *The Deer Hunter,* in 1978, and *Apocalypse Now,* a year later, highlighted these insecurities but it was another 1979 movie, *The China Syndrome,* that had the greatest impact on people's faith in corporations. Starring Jane Fonda, it told the story of a newspaper reporter who discovers a cover up about safety conditions at a nuclear power station. The movie echoed long-held concerns about nuclear power risks; just 12 days after the movie's release those risks were underscored by an accident at the Three Mile Island nuclear plant in Pennsylvania.[12]

The 1980s brought with it four of the world's worst environmental disasters and a slew of mini-scandals. In 1981 European consumer faith in olive oil was shaken when Spanish producers were accused of selling a contaminated product that killed more than 1,000 people and serious injured 25,000 others. "It was the most devastating food poisoning in modern European history," the *Guardian* wrote. Years later the scandal and cycle of blame would be compounded by new research suggesting that olive oil wasn't the real culprit but, instead, the toxic sickness had been caused by pesticides sprayed on tomatoes.[13]

In December 1984, a valve broke under pressure at the Union Carbide pesticide plant in Bhopal, India, releasing some 30 tonnes of methyl isocyanate – a highly toxic gas – into the air. More than 600,000 people were exposed to the gas cloud and at least 20,000 people required hospital treatment for symptoms that included burning eyes, frothing at the mouth and breathing difficulties. Over time some 15,000 people would die from gas-related health issues.[14]

Then, on April 26, 1986 the world's worst fears about nuclear power were realised when the main reactor exploded at the Chernobyl power plant in Ukraine (then part of the Soviet Union) sending radioactive material as far afield as the west coast of Ireland. Even though the death toll was relatively low, more than 250,000 people had to be permanently resettled and to this day a 30 kilometre exclusion zone around the reactor remains in place.

All three of these 1980s disasters fuelled a growing fear among the public that neither business nor governments cared enough about the communities that they were supposed to value and be a part of. But, in terms of awakening environmental awareness, it was the 1989 Exxon Valdez oil spill in Alaska – and the oil giant's subsequent attempts to litigate its way out of being held accountable – that really riled the public and set the tone for a new generation of activism.

When the Valdez ran aground in northern Prince William Sound, it spilled 42 million litres of crude oil and contaminated some 1,990 kilometres of shoreline. In the days immediately after the spill, an estimated 2,000 sea otters, 302 harbour seals and about 250,000 seabirds perished. The clean-up and wildlife rescue operation played out on the TV nightly news bulletins and in the newspapers and, when compensation to local people was included, would cost the company $3.4 billion.[15]

The medium starts to spreads the message

The importance of 24-hour cable TV news had been growing throughout the 1980s but it achieved new relevance during the 1990 Gulf War. Millions were glued to their TVs watching the air assaults on Baghdad in real time (and listening to CNN anchor Bernard Shaw broadcasting live from the city while under attack).

Yet the increased interest in cable news brought with it new pressures on 24-hour news organisations to "feed the beast." As a result cable news editors began searching out new sources of content and expanding their view of what was newsworthy. What once were considered purely local or regional stories now could have global resonance – especially if the themes and undercurrents spoke to similar issues elsewhere in the world.

This glocal approach to news arrived exactly at the wrong time for the Royal Dutch Shell oil company when in 1995 it attempted to "retire" one of its old oil storage platforms, the Brent Spar, by blowing it up and then sinking it in the North Sea.

Disposing of the Brent Spar in this way raised a larger issue of deep sea dumping that environmental NGO Greenpeace was eager to counter. It launched a direct action campaign against Shell including sending activists to the Brent Spar platform in the North Sea, which they boarded and then proceeded to occupy in stormy conditions for nearly a month despite coming under water cannon bombardment by Shell.

Greenpeace filmed the operation and supplied the footage to eager news organisations. Shell didn't have its own footage of the standoff so Greenpeace's side of events became the de facto storyline for the media. It also created a dedicated webpage for its Brent Spar protest at a time when Shell didn't even have a corporate site and the NGO bolstered its attacks on the oil company by claiming that the Brent Spar disposal would cause toxic and oil pollution on a massive scale (though these claims were later found to have been overstated).

Firmly in control of the narrative, Greenpeace expanded the campaign against Shell to mainland Europe including countries like the Netherlands and Germany that had a strong tradition of environmentalism.

"Greenpeace ran a highly-emotional lobbying campaign – it was well targeted, used saturation state-of-the-art TV technology, advanced public relations techniques such as a 'home page' on the Internet and a budget of over $2 million," wrote Julian Oliver, an executive at Edelman at the time.[16]

Andrew Vickers, Shell's vice-president for policy and external relations, told *Ethical Corporation* in 2010 that the decision not to sink Brent Spar was "a tipping point" for Shell, NGOs and the media. "For Shell, it was about more than Brent Spar. Overplaying the legal card, underestimating the power of modern media tools and not seeing the deeper agenda are challenges that we work hard to address."[17]

As *Ethical Corporation* concluded: "The Spar episode forcibly brought home to Shell the fact that its brand and reputation were truly global and open to influence by outside parties." In its wake, companies began to pay far closer attention to crisis management and to stakeholder engagement. Out of this, many corporate social responsibility and accountability practices eventually emerged.

Brent Spar was a wake-up call for both corporations and activists alike to the power of the Internet and digital organising. While in the past NGOs might have relied on phone banks to motivate their supporters, they now turned to new technologies like email and Listserv campaigns to mobilise support and outrage.

Books like *Netactivism*, published in 1996, provided a hands-on guide for NGOs to mobilise using email and other Internet tools. In one powerful example from 1999, California-based NGO Rainforest Action Network rapidly mobilised support using email organising for a remote Colombian indigenous community, the U'Wa, whose land was threatened by the US oil company Occidental Petroleum.[18]

Activism goes mobile

By the late 1990s society's ability to connect, communicate and collaborate en masse had taken on another dimension. Thanks to the advances in cellular phone technology and the network coverage infrastructure that enabled this, millions of people could now connect via telephone, text or email – even when they were outside of the home or the office. Many people in the growing economies of Asia, South America, Middle East and North Africa would come to depend solely on mobile networks as landline infrastructure didn't exist.

Looking back now, it's hard to conceive just how transformative the mobile phone was in the 1990s. Having your own dedicated phone number (and by extension your own personal data trail) opened up new avenues in personalised services. With the advent of mobile web connectivity – first seen in a consumer device with the Nokia Communicator in 1996 – people began to grasp the possibilities of what mobile technology could deliver in terms of information and commerce.

Many of the online services such as food and grocery delivery, music sharing and streaming and even banking we now take for granted (and access through our smartphones) were first envisaged during the dot-com boom of the late 1990s. A lot of those ideas failed at the time purely because the Internet and mobile phone infrastructure couldn't match the scale of the digital ideas being conjured by the bright minds in Silicon Valley and beyond.

Social activism wasn't dependent on massive bandwidth however – it was the essence of mobilising through online connectivity that helped it thrive. The 1999 World Trade Organisation protests in Seattle were coordinated through a series of activist websites. Two years later anti-government protesters in the Philippines gathered en masse thanks to mobile phone organising – one of the first examples of what writer Howard Rheingold described as smart mobs in his 2002 book of the same name. Texting on cellphones allowed people to behave in the same intelligent "emergent behaviour" seen in swarms of bees – namely by forming into a group controlled by no single person, yet moving as if having a mind of its own. Now, people could "act together in new ways and in situations where collective action was not possible before," Rheingold wrote.[19]

The network effect changes the game

Digital connectivity allowed activists to organise and mobilise faster than ever before. Yet, for the most part, NGOs were still communicating with their core base of supporters or other like-minded groups. It would take the viral power of instant sharing offered by social networks to supercharge opinion and outrage about corporate and governmental wrongdoing. Not surprisingly, given their prior knowledge of email, mobile and web-based organising, it would be the activist community that would weaponise social media conversation to fight big business.

Facebook was already on course to become the world's most powerful social network and a major disruptive force in the relationship between brands and the rest of society. But in terms of environmental and social activism, YouTube had the greatest initial impact, and no NGO used the video social network to better effect than Greenpeace.

On March 30, 2007 a video was posted to YouTube titled *Kleenex Gets Punk'd!*[20] It showed a clandestine agitprop stunt by Greenpeace activists to pressure the Kimberly-Clark Corporation to stop sourcing paper products from boreal forests in the Pacific North-West.

The YouTube video depicted just one part of the campaign – a direct-action event to spoof and disrupt the filming of a sappy Kleenex TV advert about how good it is to cry – and it wasn't even uploaded from an official Greenpeace account. Nevertheless the video soon had racked up more than 300,000 views – a paltry figure by today's viewing standards but an impressive reach at a time when few videos hit the million viewer mark on the young social network.

The multi-year "Kleercut" campaign would ultimately result in Kimberly-Clark committing to new sustainable forest sourcing standards and a landmark partnership between the corporation and the NGO to help maintain sustainability standards.

Greenpeace's YouTube experiment showed how direct-action tactics could now reach the masses through social media, prompting viewers who might never have called themselves "green" to start asking questions about where the products they were buying came from and what was the process that made them. But it wasn't until one year later, when Greenpeace applied its new social media activism strategy against Unilever, that the full-force of social media activism became clear.

At the time, Unilever brand Dove had just released a new advert called *Onslaught,* part of the Real Beauty self-esteem campaign (discussed in greater detail in Chapter 7). As *Ad Age* described the Dove ad at the time; "In one brief minute, it indicts the culture's obsession with Barbie-doll exteriors, raises the consciousness of girls and women and exposes the inner ugliness of the so-called beauty industry."[21]

Yet even as Unilever received kudos for its stand on female self-esteem it was facing growing criticism on another major sustainability issue – the sourcing of palm oil, an essential ingredient in many of the company's products.

In April 2008 Greenpeace released a highly critical report, *How Unilever Palm Oil Suppliers Are Burning up Borneo.* It documented:

> further evidence of the expansion of the palm oil sector in Indonesia into remaining rainforests, orang-utan habitat and peatlands in Kalimantan [and] It link[ed] the majority of the largest producers in Indonesia to Unilever, probably the largest palm oil corporate consumer in the world.[22]

Greenpeace accompanied the publication of the report with direct-action campaigning including sending activists dressed up in orang-utan outfits to protest outside Unilever corporate offices. But it was a slick protest video – a dark parody of *Onslaught* – posted on YouTube that delivered the most impact.

Greenpeace's version was titled *Onslaughter* and its target was the palm oil sourcing practices of Dove and parent company Unilever. The video showed the clear-cutting of tropical forests in Indonesia and Malaysia to make way for palm oil plantations, and the threat this industrial cultivation had on local people and wildlife, notably the endangered orang-utan population.[23]

Prominent in the video was a young girl, Azizah, whose home was under threat from palm oil production. While the original Dove self-esteem advert ended with the line: "Talk to your daughter before the beauty industry does," Greenpeace's video ended this way: "98% of Indonesia's lowland forest will be gone by the time Azizah is 25. Most is destroyed to make palm oil, which is used in Dove products. Talk to Dove before it is too late."

The consumer outrage on YouTube took Unilever by surprise. As Greenpeace wrote in an analysis of the palm oil campaign on its own website:

> In just two weeks the company had received tens of thousands of protest emails from around the world, seen Greenpeace activists bring hoards of news media to their buildings in the United Kingdom, Netherlands and Italy, and watched our viral video "Dove Onslaught(er)" take off faster than anything we've ever done before. Public pressure moved them.[24]

The upshot was that, in early May 2008, Unilever and Greenpeace sat down to address the NGO's allegations. By the end of the discussions Unilever agreed to support an immediate moratorium on deforestation for palm oil in South East Asia; use its leadership role within the consumer goods sector to "aggressively" build a coalition of companies to support the moratorium; and put pressure on its palm oil suppliers in Indonesia as well as the Indonesian government to support the moratorium.[25]

As Greenpeace put it, "Not bad for two 2 weeks campaigning!"

Unilever maintained that it was aware of and already addressing the palm oil sourcing concerns before Greenpeace got involved. Still, there was no denying the impact that the NGO's social media bully pulpit had on one of the world's largest companies. The power of viral video campaigning sent shock waves through the corporate social responsibility and corporate communication departments of the world's major corporations and appeared to surprise even Greenpeace's own campaigners. The social media experiment had paid off better than even they could have imagined and emboldened the NGO to expand the palm oil campaign while providing a blueprint for a new generation of social media–led campaigning.

As Greenpeace warned on its website in the aftermath of the Unilever campaign: "If others in the palm oil industry are smart, they'll follow Unilever's lead. There's no excuse for wasting time now, so any industry slow-learners could be our next campaign target."

Greenpeace wasn't joking. Over the next three years it would embark on a series of high-profile palm oil social media campaigns against major corporations and brands including Burger King and, most notably, Kit Kat in a bruising encounter that sullied the Nestlé's brand reputation for many months (and which is discussed in more depth in Chapter 3).

Bringing sustainability to the masses

From the activist *Sturm und Drang* delivered by the likes of Greenpeace, it would be tempting to conclude that the corporate world couldn't have cared less about environmental and social issues at the birth of the social media age. The reality was far more nuanced.

Certainly some companies demonstrated an egregious disregard for the planet and society but, by 2005, many major organisations were already exploring the business advantages of energy saving, recycling and sustainable sourcing. Unilever, for example, had been a founding member of the Roundtable on Sustainable Palm Oil (a collaboration between industry and the World Wildlife Fund) back in 2002. Others, like Danone and Nestlé, were investing in new sustainable agriculture practices and partnerships to cut costs and secure long-term access to materials and natural resources. Some companies – Nike, for example (as explored in Chapter 5) – had paid a steep price in terms of lost credibility and sales for unsustainable business practices in the 1990s and were keen to make amends in order to rebuild a battered reputation.

The roots of the modern corporate sustainability movement can be traced back to the early 1970s when governments and NGOs (the United Nations in particular) began to tackle just how our world could prosper when faced with concerns around population growth, food security, malnutrition, resource scarcity and yes, even back then, climate change. They were joined by new ecological economic thinkers such as E.F. Schumacher (author of *Small is Beautiful*) and Amory Lovins (co-founder of the Rocky Mountain Institute), who embraced the progress made by the environmental movement but added a key economic component to their worldview.[26] If sustainability was going to reshape the world it couldn't operate in isolation from the forces of capitalism that powered that world and, despite its many glaring problems, capitalism had also been responsible for an enormous increase in the global standard of living over the past century.

The evolving philosophy of business being a driver for environmental and social progress sounded good, but it required a framework that could unite both sustainability do-gooders and hard-nosed number crunchers. Karl-Henrik Robert, a cancer researcher by profession, got the intellectual ball rolling with *The Natural Step*, his four-part analysis of the conditions needed to guaranteed a sustainable society. Then, in 1997, businessman and sustainability seer John Elkington published *Cannibals with Forks: The Triple Bottom Line of 21st Century Business*. It offered a new rationale for measuring corporate value by taking into account not just profit, but also people and the planet.

Elkington's concept made common pact with a series of new reporting and measurement standards – such as the Global Reporting Initiative and the Climate Disclosure Project – designed to make business more accountable for its sustainability footprint.

Admittedly, the corporate world wasn't exactly in a rush to put sustainability at the heart of business strategy. But, over the next decade, a new generation of sustainability-savvy employees combined with the external cajoling by investors, the media and NGOs, persuaded more and more companies to start calculating the economic value of being environmentally and socially responsible.

That wasn't too difficult to demonstrate when it came to cutting energy and raw material costs but placing an economic value on a company's impact on the world (what economists like to call "externalities") was a tougher proposition – especially in an age where stock price and the ability to deliver a regular dividend to shareholders had come to be seen as the true measure of a company's value and worth.

Gradually though, some companies started to re-evaluate how they needed to measure long-term success as they came to terms with growing outside pressures about social and environmental responsibilities as well as a heightened understanding of the major demographic, technological and economic trends shaping 21st-century society.

The insurance industry was at the forefront of mapping climate change and extreme weather risk in the early 2000s and these efforts were increased following Hurricane Katrina in 2005. The banking sector, meanwhile, was alive to the growth opportunities in the new microfinance business – especially given how new technologies like mobile phones could help drive adoption in emerging markets. At the same time, the rapid expansion of technology and connectivity in modern society, combined with a mass migration from the rural areas into new urban centres, was causing entire sectors – from automobiles to utilities to consumer electronics and technology – to question the sustainability of their future business planning.

Yet despite all this internal activity, sustainability still wasn't considered sexy enough for marketing or public relations to worry too much about. Sustainability was viewed as a technical or a fringe topic that only outside environmentalists would really care about. Brand marketers found it hard to grasp that the very issues sustainability teams were concerned about – sourcing, supply chain, minimising toxic ingredients and improving labour conditions – could resonate with consumers. Once again, social media would demonstrate just how important sustainability issues were to the public and what a serious risk to a company's reputation they posed.

The rise of Mommy Bloggers

Millions of individual social media users have helped amplify the concerns raised by social and environmental activists but, in the early days of social media no subculture had more clout than the so-called Mommy Bloggers.

Personal goods giant Johnson & Johnson was first to be on the receiving end of Mommy Blogger wrath in 2008 when some decided that an advertising campaign for its painkiller brand, Motrin, was demeaning to mothers. Within hours of the advert being released online a network of Mommy bloggers called for a boycott of Motrin. As *The New York Times'* own mother-focused blog, Motherlode, reported:

> By Sunday afternoon a few bloggers and tweeters had gotten the ad agency that created the ad on the phone, to find they didn't know a lot about Twitter and didn't seem to have a clue that there was so much anger piling up online.[27]

The company found itself apologising and recut the advert.

Then, in 2009 the Campaign for Safe Cosmetics – a coalition of NGOs including Friends of the Earth, Health Care Without Harm, Clean Water Fund and Commonweal – issued a damning report titled *No More Toxic Tub* that analysed 48 baby care products including Johnson's iconic Baby Shampoo. The report found that 61 percent of the products tested contained the carcinogens formaldehyde and 1,4-dioxane.

The report received widespread media attention and gained momentum through a coordinated letter writing campaign by more than 40 organisations representing 1.7 million parents, health care providers and environmental health advocates. It was bolstered and reinforced by relentless social media attacks on Johnson & Johnson brands' Facebook pages by concerned Mommy Bloggers.

The company was adamant that its products were safe for people of all ages to use but it had underestimated the level of consumers' shock and suspicion about what chemicals they might be subjected to. Ultimately the company agreed to develop new formulas for its baby products and those sold through its other major brands such as Neutrogena, Aveeno and Clean & Clear.

In a blog post, Susan Nettesheim, vice president for product integrity and toxicology, explained the decision:

> Over the past few years, some interest groups have raised questions about the ingredients in personal care products used widely around the world, and they've put particular focus on our baby products. At first we were disappointed, because we know that all our products are safe by scientific standards and meet or exceed government regulations. Over time, though, we've come to realise that sometimes safety alone isn't enough.[28]

The Mommy Blogger movement demonstrated loudly and quite painfully for brands that the public very much cared about sustainability issues. It was just that they didn't talk in the technical terms sustainability professionals liked to use. Instead, they talked about sustainability in terms of how the issues related to their own families and community.

At the heart of this awareness and interest in sustainability was social media, of course. Now consumers were regularly calling out companies on social media not just for bad customer service or malfunctioning products but also for their position on a range of environmental and social sustainability issues. Yet most companies were on a steep learning curve in how they interacted with social media communities. Many still laboured under the mistaken notion that they controlled the conversation online – a hangover of 100 years spent manipulating the message.

As we'll see in the next chapter, this mindset created serious communication and customer relations problems – ones that companies continue to fall foul of even today.

Notes

1   www.crf-usa.org/bill-of-rights-in-action/bria-24-1-b-upton-sinclairs-the-jungle-muckraking-the-meat-packing-industry.html
2   www.theguardian.com/books/2006/aug/05/featuresreviews.guardianreview24
3   www.wired.com/2013/01/looney-gas-and-lead-poisoning-a-short-sad-history/
4   https://en.wikipedia.org/wiki/Silent_Spring
5   James Ridgeway was a colleague and mentor during my years working at the *Village Voice* newspaper.
6   http://auto.howstuffworks.com/1971-1980-ford-pinto12.htm
7   www.nybooks.com/articles/2010/06/10/food-movement-rising/
8   Brigitte Sebastia (2017). *Eating Traditional Food: Politics, Identity and Practices*. London: Routledge
9   www.thedailybeast.com/articles/2015/04/15/the-bad-business-of-baby-food.html
10 https://www.theguardian.com/sustainable-business/nestle-baby-milk-scandal-food-industry-standards
11 www.adcouncil.org/Our-Campaigns/The-Classics/Pollution-Keep-America-Beautiful-Iron-Eyes-Cody
12 www.nytimes.com/2007/09/16/magazine/16wwln-freakonomics-t.html
13 www.theguardian.com/education/2001/aug/25/research.highereducation
14 http://news.bbc.co.uk/onthisday/hi/dates/stories/december/3/newsid_2698000/2698709.stm
15 https://www.scientificamerican.com/article/environmental-effects-of/
16 www.politico.eu/article/learning-the-lessons-of-brent-spar-saga/
17 www.ethicalcorp.com/business-strategy/brent-spar-battle-launched-modern-activism
18 www.salon.com/1999/03/19/newsb_69/
19 www.nytimes.com/2002/12/15/magazine/the-year-in-ideas-smart-mobs.html
20 www.youtube.com/watch?v=sZCym0DB7hA
21 http://adage.com/article/ad-review/dove-s-onslaught-ad-a-triumph/120975/
22 www.greenpeace.org/international/en/publications/reports/how-unilever-palm-oil-supplier/
23 www.youtube.com/watch?v=odI7pQFyjso
24 www.greenpeace.org/international/en/campaigns/forests/asia-pacific/dove-palmoil-action/
25 www.greenpeace.org/international/en/campaigns/forests/asia-pacific/dove-palmoil-action/
26 Jeremy L. Caradonna (2014). *Sustainability: A History*. New York: Oxford University Press, p. 113.
27 https://parenting.blogs.nytimes.com/2008/11/17/moms-and-motrin/
28 www.npr.org/sections/health-shots/2012/08/15/158832173/johnson-johnson-pledges-to-purge-controversial-chemicals

Chapter 3

Learning to listen after a century of shouting

Having spent the best part of a century distancing themselves from the public, companies suddenly found themselves dragged into the middle of the new social media universe and being held to account for their activities. The experience was deeply uncomfortable for brands that were used to influencing consumers from a distance through TV advertising and discourse through public relations. The discombobulation was even more acute for business-to-business companies that had little if any experience dealing directly with the public.

In the past, when reputation problems arose, companies worried about what the newspapers (and maybe TV news) would report, but at least they knew those media organisations had set publishing schedules and so they had time to prepare their corporate response even as their public relations teams worked on persuading journalists that the problem wasn't as bad as it might first appear. Cable TV and the advent of the 24-hour news cycle increased the pressure on the world of brand and corporate public relations during a crisis but, even then, they knew who they were dealing with and could focus their resources accordingly.

Social media sent the old public relations world spinning off its axis of power. In terms of corporate structure, business thinking, process and talent the vast majority of companies were woefully unprepared for the fast-moving, viral and uncontrollable power that bloggers, tweeters, Facebookers and You-Tubers now possessed. Even today, in many major companies, corporate policy bans access to social networks out of concern over employee productivity.[1]

As with so many of the other disruptive megatrends with which companies struggle to come to terms, social media presented a philosophical challenge that most people in business had not encountered before: they no longer controlled the message.

The predicament of so many brands was summed up perfectly in 2006 when a couple of self-described "mad scientists" started a YouTube channel called Eepy Bird and began broadcasting a series of "experiments" that demonstrated the combustible effects of adding Mento mints to litre bottles of Diet Coke. One of the most memorable videos created a Las Vegas-style waterfall show using erupting Diet Coke bottles.

Coca-Cola's management were unimpressed, to say the least, complaining to the *Wall Street Journal* that the experiments didn't "fit the brand personality" of Diet Coke. However, the Italian company behind the Mentos mint brand embraced the YouTube viral hits, noting that the videos were worth about $10 million in free advertising. Coca-Cola would also soon see the light. As the company's vice-president of global interactive marketing later admitted: "The biggest takeaway [from the Diet Coke-Mentos video] was consumers own our brands."[2]

More than a decade on from Coca-Cola's eureka moment other brands still struggle. Every year, companies find themselves caught in a social media storm. Sometimes it's because of their tin-eared approach to the public's problems. Other times they are blindsided by real-world events and crises that then are amplified and magnified by the global megaphone that is social media.

However and whenever they occur, these social media mistakes can have a very serious impact on a company's reputation and, from time to time, its bottom line. In terms of building trust with consumers and greater society, a social media crisis is the online equivalent of kryptonite on Superman – it can paralyse a business in an instant and leave it severely weakened and compromised for months to come.

The lessons not learned

Over the past 15 years there have been countless examples of corporate social media mistakes. Some are quite trivial while others have posed a real threat to the business. Nearly all of them, however, fall into these categories of mistakes and miscalculations.

Companies don't listen or underestimate new platforms

The first chapter of this book discussed how the bike lock company, Kryptonite, misjudged the impact that a negative blog post could have on its business because it underestimated the power of the new publishing technology. The mistake cost Kryptonite millions of dollars but, in terms of social media faux pas, the company is hardly alone – many other companies have repeated its misjudgement in the years that have followed.

Take the case of Target. In 2008, four years after the Kryptonite case and a lifetime in social media history, the retailer made exactly the same mistake. That winter, Target had launched a new billboard advertising campaign featuring a fully clothed female model making what appeared to be a snow angel superimposed on the back of a large Target logo.

It was just the sort of innocuous inane billboard you might see every day walking around New York. To Amy Jussel, founder and executive director of Shaping Youth, however, the spread-eagled pose of the model was "sexualized ad slop" as she ranted in her blog. And that's where the issue might have faded away had Jussel not also reached out to Target for comment.

Many companies might not have bothered to respond. Target probably wishes it hadn't either, for what it wrote took what was a non-issue and turned it into a full-blown social media storm.

The reply was succinct but not terribly satisfying for Jussel and her blog: "Thank you for contacting Target; unfortunately we are unable to respond to your inquiry because Target does not participate with non-traditional media outlets."[3] Ouch.

When Jussel blogged Target's response the "blogosphere" – yes, that is what people called it back then – erupted. After all, there were well over 100 million active blogs by 2008 and Jussel was well connected in the Mommy and marketing blog world. These bloggers started ridiculing Target for ignoring blogs and not respecting its own customers. And, just as happened with Kryptonite, a reporter from *The New York Times* also was paying attention. By the time they reached Target for comment about the social media uproar the retailer was already regretting its stance. "We do not work with bloggers currently [but] we are reviewing the policy and may adjust it," Target sheepishly told the *Times*[4].

It seems hard to imagine now but there was a time when even Facebook could be underestimated. In 2007, HSBC initially failed to grasp a consumer protest against new student fees that was developing on the social media platform. That summer the bank had quietly introduced a new set of overdraft fees for recent university graduates in the United Kingdom. A few responded by launching the "Stop the Great HSBC Graduate Rip-Off!" Facebook group. As more than 3,000 fellow students joined in over the first few days, the Facebook group quickly became one of the most effective social media pressure campaigns seen at the time. Central to its impact was the fact that journalists could quantify the size of the protest by the numbers joining the group and quote those figures in their stories.

The Facebook protest took HSBC by surprise – at the time the network wasn't exactly known as a hotbed for consumer agitation – but it didn't take long for the bank to grasp the seriousness of the protest (especially when UK newspapers started covering it). Within one month of the page being set up the students had forced HSBC to withdraw the new fee structure. As the BBC wrote at the time, the now famous U-turn proved HSBC "was not too big to listen to its customers".[5]

A social media slap in the face for one of the world's biggest banks would make the entire industry take note nowadays yet three years after HSBC's bank fee fiasco Bank of America committed the same mistake. In the summer of 2011, online consumer forums were abuzz about a rumoured $5 monthly surcharge that BofA was planning for debit cardholders. Critics complained that the bank (having received some $45 billion in federal bailout funds just a few years before) was being insensitive to account holders at a time when the US economy was struggling. Despite growing levels of online and social media outrage the bank management went ahead with the plan. The backlash was swift offline and online.

There were protests outside bank branches in Los Angeles, Miami and San Francisco, and TV talk show hosts Jay Leno and Ellen Degeneres ridiculed BofA for its heartlessness. Even President Barack Obama blasted the fee. One customer launched an online petition on Change.org that attracted 306,000 signatures in just a few days. Soon after, BofA dropped the fee – something it should have done months earlier had it correctly gauged the level of customer outrage being vented via social media.

Then there were the companies that didn't listen to Twitter. In the summer of 2008 not many Fortune 500 companies used the platform. There certainly weren't many big energy companies tweeting. It was really quite innovative then for ExxonMobil to embrace the medium as it appeared to do in August of that year with the launch of @Exxonmobilcorp – and all the more surprising given that one of its first tweets was a pledge to reduce greenhouse gas emissions by 3 percent despite its previous scepticism about global warming. It was only when the *Houston Chronicle* called ExxonMobil for comment in regard to a feature it was writing about Twitter that the corporation learned it had been "brand-jacked".[6]

Not grasping the power of Twitter back in 2008 was perhaps understandable. Less so was BP's failure to pay attention to the social network as it undertook a mammoth damage limitation and reputation salvage operation in the wake of the 2010 Deepwater Horizon disaster. Eleven people died in the oil exploration blowout and more than 6,000 birds perished as millions of gallons of oil spilled into the Gulf of Mexico, affecting 1,000 miles of shoreline.

In the first three months after the spill, BP spent an estimated $60 million in crisis communication efforts including TV and press ads as well as a sophisticated online search campaign. Despite this investment BP neglected to pay attention to Twitter and Facebook so, when a Los Angeles–based comedian called Josh Simpson set up the @BPGlobalPR Twitter and started tweeting acerbic and withering commentary about the supermajor, BP was in the dark even as the spoof account gained 18,000 followers in just a few days. Yet again, it was only when the media asked BP's communications team about the account that the company realised it had been made a fool of.

The Twitter spoof was embarrassing for BP but, ultimately, it was the wake-up call the company needed in order to upgrade its communication strategy for the social media age. Within weeks BP was investing heavily in both Twitter and Facebook to try and repair its standing with local communities and the US public in general.

Companies mistake marketing for authentic conversation

In 2006, Walmart was beset by a public relations backlash over its labour relations policy – this included a federal lawsuit that sought to reclaim $33.5 million in employee overtime back pay. The world's biggest retailer was also fighting a Chicago city ordinance that aimed to raise the minimum wage.

Not everyone was beating up on Walmart, though. A writer/photographer couple, Laura and Jim, had recently started a travel blog called Wal-Marting Across America. In the blog they shared heart-warming tales of exploring the nation in a Winnebago and paid tribute to the friendly Walmart employees who let them stay for free each night in a store car park.

If this social media portrait of Walmart's benevolence seemed a little too good to be true, well, it was. After a few days online sleuthing by anti-Walmart activists, it transpired that Laura and Jim's cross country trip was being funded by a public relations agency, Edelman. One of their biggest clients was, you guessed it, Walmart.

Edelman's fake blog would become a cautionary lesson for every brand and agency trying to communicate through social media. The old advertising ethos that creative storytelling was more important than being honest with the public no longer stood up now that the public had the power to uncover and call out the deception. The lesson was particularly painful because it showed how even chief executives couldn't hide from criticism. Edelman's founder, Richard Edelman, had made a point of embracing social media and making himself accessible through a daily blog he wrote. In the wake of the Walmart fiasco he was forced to personally answer hundreds of angry comments, admitting: "I want to acknowledge our error in failing to be transparent about the identity of the two bloggers from the outset. This is 100% our responsibility and our error; not the client's."[7]

At least Edelman and Walmart had the good grace not to muscle into geopolitics and civil strife. That's the mistake British retailer Habitat made in 2009 when some youthful, over-eager social media marketer hijacked a trending Twitter hashtag #Mousavi – set up to support democratic protests against the results of the Iranian presidential election – to promote Habitat's "totally desirable Spring collection". Faced with immediate social media rebuke and ridicule, Habitat deleted the tweets and apologised before shutting down the account. A few months later it relaunched with a more experienced social media team.

Habitat's Twitter faux pas generated such a volume of coverage among the marketing and business community that you'd assume no brand would ever make the same mistake. Yet just two years later Kenneth Cole did just that promoting its new Spring collection with the #Cairo hashtag during the bloody Tahrir Square uprising of the 2011 Arab Spring. This time Kenneth Cole couldn't blame the mistake on some junior underling, because the offending tweet – "Millions are in uproar in #Cairo. Rumour is they heard our new spring collection is available online." – was sent by none other than founder Kenneth Cole himself.

Consumers have the clout

By 2008 the potential of social media to both help and harm was known by every major consumer-facing brand in the United States and Europe. There were dedicated blogs, online magazines and entire conferences dedicated to covering this business and cultural shift.[8] Yet, despite the growing body of marketing and public relations case studies highlighting the power connected consumers could wield, some of the biggest companies still couldn't comprehend how their world had changed – none more so than United Airlines.

In March 2008, Dave Carroll, a member of an obscure Canadian folk rock band, Sons of Maxwell, was flying with United Airlines when his favourite guitar was badly damaged in transit. One passenger claimed that baggage handlers in Chicago had been throwing the guitar around. Over the next year Carroll attempted to seek $1,200 in compensation but was brushed back by United customer service. Finally, out of frustration, Carroll turned to creative protest, recording a music video titled *United Breaks Guitars* and posting it on YouTube.

Carroll's complaint went viral almost overnight with 1.5 million views in the first four days and 4 million in the first month. As the media started paying attention to the video, United's share price also took a $180 million hit (though there's no concrete evidence Carroll's song was the cause). Having rebuffed Carroll for the best part of a year, United now tried to protect its reputation by promising to pay the cost of repairing the guitar and offering Carroll flight vouchers worth $1,200. "They definitely want this to go away," he told the *Guardian*.[9]

Other consumers had started creative musical protests before Carroll's song. A year earlier Lloyds Banking Group had been the subject of a YouTube-powered musical attack over bank charges titled *I Fought the Lloyds* that made the UK Top 40 singles chart.[10] But *United Breaks Guitars* had a much larger impact because it tapped into a groundswell of consumer grievances against the airline industry in general and United in particular. Carroll's complaint became powerful not only because of its attention-grabbing creativity but also because United Airlines failed to grasp that interesting content the public can identify with stood a good chance of going viral.

Greenpeace already understood just how powerful consumer clout could be, having successfully run social media campaigns against Unilever and Kimberly-Clark. In 2011 it took aim at Nestlé by staging one of the very first brand-jackings of a Facebook page: Kit Kat.

Greenpeace created an altered Kit Kat logo that read "Nestlé Killer" – the contention being that every Kit Kat chocolate bar bought was contributing to the destruction of orangutan habitats in Indonesia – and encouraged its supporters to post the logo on Kit Kat's 90,000 strong Facebook page.

The "Nestlé Killer" logos, along with mounting protest posts on its Facebook fan page proved too much for the food giant to ignore. In what would prove to be a major communication mistake, the brand responded to the protest posts by writing: "We welcome your comments, but please don't post using an altered version of any of our logos as your profile pic – they will be deleted."[11]

To many Facebook users and social media commentators, Kit Kat was stifling free speech.[12] The volume of anger on the brand's page intensified as more and more people became "fans" simply to protest. With its Kit Kat Facebook page in total meltdown, Nestlé decided it should apologise to its fans for deleting posts. By then, though, the Greenpeace campaign had gone global. Within a month of the first comments posted to Facebook, Nestlé's chairman, Peter Brabeck-Letmathe, agreed to cut all ties with dubious palm oil producers and to have The Forest Trust audit its palm oil sourcing in the future.

You can't control the crowd

To the world of marketing, crowdsourcing must have looked like a godsend (see more discussion in Chapter 4). Why waste all that money on advertising and public relations when social media communities can spread the word for free? There was just one problem. Getting the public to talk about a product was easy. Ensuring that conversation was positive was impossible, as General Motors (GM) would soon discover. In 2006, with crowdsourced online sites like Wikipedia getting mainstream attention, GM's Chevrolet brand launched an online contest encouraging the public to create a TV ad for a new version of its Tahoe SUV. Chevrolet provided the video clips and background music for the ad. All the contestants had to do was mix the material and add their own captions before sharing the final results on the brand's website.

Some 30,000 people took part in the competition and a great deal of positive brand-friendly content was created. But it was the vocal minority of anti-SUV campaigners that stood out as they submitted entries with captions such as: "Global Warming is Here", "$70 to Fill Up the Tank" and "Enjoy the Longer Summers!" – an indictment of the Tahoe's gas-guzzling impact on global warming. As *Wired* wrote in one of the many media autopsies of this car crash of a social media campaign: "On its own Web site, the Tahoe now stood accused of everything but running down the Pillsbury Doughboy."[13]

And that, you would have thought, would have been the end of crowdsourced brand marketing campaigns. After all, companies were having a hard enough time handling all the consumer gripes being levelled at them through social media without creating a ready-made vehicle to get run over with.

The reality, of course, was quite different. Companies had controlled the message through advertising and public relations for so long that they found it difficult to believe that their own crowdsourced brand campaign could end badly even when they saw other companies suffer at the hands of the crowd.

In early 2012 McDonald's found itself similarly under attack as a result of its #McDStories Twitter hashtag campaign. Extolling Twitter users to recount their favourite stories about eating at McDonald's, people did just that, taking the company to task for its nutritional claims, the taste of its burgers and its ethical treatment of animals. At least McDonald's was quick to spot there were problems. "Within an hour, we saw that it wasn't going as planned," McDonald's social media director Rick Wion told PaidContent.org. "It was negative enough that we set about a change of course."[14]

The same year UK retailer Waitrose got more than it bargained for when it tried the same "tell us what you think of us" crowdsourced marketing. But the humorous ribbing the supermarket retailer received about representing upper middle-class privilege was mild compared to the abuse aimed at JPMorgan Chase & Co. a year later when it too succumbed to the lure of crowdsourced compliments and hosted a Twitter chat about careers in banking with vice-chairman Jimmy Lee using the hashtag #AskJPM.[15]

Given that JPMorgan had just been fined $920 million dollars for its "London Whale" trading loss, and given that it had also just agreed to a $13 billion settlement with the US Justice Department over bad mortgage loans stemming from the 2008 financial crash, it wasn't entirely clear why the normally very conservative bank considered an open-ended Twitter chat such a good idea.

It soon regretted the decision as Lee was inundated with a torrent of sarcastic and some downright abusive comments and questions – almost none of them about careers. A *New Yorker* post, succinctly titled "JP Morgan's Twitter Mistake," recounted these humdingers that the bank had to field: "Did you always want to be part of a vast, corrupt criminal enterprise or did you 'break bad'?"; "Did you have a specific number of people's lives you needed to ruin before you considered your business model a success?"; "What section of the poor & disenfranchised have you yet to exploit for profit, & how are you working to address that?"; and "When [CEO] Jamie Dimon eats babies are they served rare? I understand anything above medium-rare is considered gauche." Chastised, JP Morgan's own social media team went quiet. The next week they tweeted: "Tomorrow's Q&A is cancelled. Bad Idea. Back to the drawing board."[16]

Consumer protests will be televised (sort of)

Nowadays, you can be sure that when something bad happens it's going to be captured on camera and shared via social media. If the issue is serious enough, the social media response will be so loud that mainstream media organisations will also pay attention – and, before you know it, what was an isolated incident is getting replayed all over the world with potential geopolitical consequences for the company or brand in question. Simply put, to paraphrase the legendary American football commentator Chris Berman, you can't stop a social media firestorm, you can only hope to contain it.

What companies can't be is tin-eared, arrogant and defensive – all the negative qualities United Airlines exhibited in April 2017 when it forcibly removed one paying passenger because it wanted his seat for one of its own employees. The incident in Chicago – United's main hub in the United States – resulted in David Dao, a 69-year old doctor from Kentucky, being dragged off the plane, suffering two broken teeth, a broken jaw, a concussion and a bloody nose in the process. The episode was captured and shared with the world via another passenger's mobile phone, of course. Tyler Bridges, the passenger who posted a video to Twitter, told *The New York Times*: "It felt like something the world needed to see."[17]

United's response was straight out of a defensive pre-social media crisis communication handbook. First it claimed the passenger had been disruptive and belligerent. Then CEO Oscar Munoz doubled down on the criticism by publicly blaming Dao despite the fact that the assault on the passenger had gone viral on social media for all the world to see. Within days United had back-pedalled and admitted fault. By then the airline's reputation was in tatters, with some Asian consumers threatening a boycott and everyone from late-night talk show hosts to international politicians taking pot shots.

Two weeks later United agreed to settle with Dao for an undisclosed fee and issued new policies designed to stop this type of incident ever happening again. In a highly critical in-house investigation, the airline would later reflect that, "it had allowed internal policies to distract from the need to treat passengers with dignity and respect."[18] And, in testimony to the US Congress in the wake of the incident, Munoz admitted that the entire episode had been a "mistake of epic proportions".[19]

The insane aspect of the United incident was that the company and the airline industry as a whole have been acutely aware for nearly a decade about the reputation damage caused by video footage shared direct via social media.

As far back as 2007 Jet Blue found itself in the glare of video consumer criticism when one of its planes was grounded at New York's JFK airport during a snowstorm. Despite being in sight of the terminal building, the passengers were forced to stay on the stationary plane for more than 11 hours. A few, newly social media savvy ones vented their frustration via blogs and YouTube.

The only saving grace for Jet Blue CEO, David Neeleman, was that Twitter (founded a few months before) had yet to go mainstream. Nevertheless, he understood just how damaging the social media fallout could become and so reacted quickly offering immediate refunds and travel vouchers. Five days after the event, Neeleman unveiled a new Customer Bill of Rights[20] that required the airline to provide vouchers or refunds when things go wrong.

Neeleman also posted a video apology direct to YouTube – widely seen as the first of its kind and a de facto acknowledgment that social media channels were not just some dalliance for the Millennial generation that corporate executives could ignore. His YouTube mea culpa would be repeated in 2011 by FedEx after home video surveillance footage emerged of a FedEx employee delivering a new computer monitor by throwing it over a set of railings even though the recipient was at home at the time.

That video on YouTube prompted other FedEx customers to complain about delivery standards and even dragged rival UPS into the fray as fresh footage was posted by other users showing its drivers treating customer packages with disdain. Within days of the smashed monitor incident (and 8 million views later) FedEx's vice-president of US operations, Matthew Thornton posted a video apology:

> I want you to know that I was upset, embarrassed, and very sorry for our customer's poor experience. This goes directly against everything we have always taught our people and expect of them. It was just very disappointing.[21]

Thornton shared the bad delivery video internally to raise awareness with employees of their responsibilities and pledged to build the social media lessons into future employee training programmes.

Will companies ever stop making social media mistakes? Certainly, there are fewer examples today of bone-headed behaviour than there were in the infancy of Facebook, YouTube and Twitter. Yet, as United Airlines demonstrates, it's not the social media technology or platform that causes companies to screw up. Rather it's the internal corporate culture that continues to treat consumers as numbers or abstract objects rather than real people who deserve respect. Every business, after all, depends on satisfying consumer demand. The company or brand that alienates its consumers will not survive for long. So how, in this often brutal social media world, can companies and brands win the respect of consumers who will no longer be treated, to paraphrase Patrick McGoohan, as numbers anymore?

That's what Part 2 of this book will explore.

Notes

1 In 2013 I was providing social media crisis consulting for one company after a consumer activist group launched a protest. Based on Twitter conversations I could see that the protesters had started marching on the head office of the company – but no-one in the company knew because social media access was banned. It was only after that I alerted the public relations department that they could, in turn, alert security of the protest.

2   http://www.adweek.com/digital/coca-cola-hunts-social-net-formula-95377/
3   https://www.prweek.com/article/1254183/target-mulls-media-policy-shift
4   http://www.nytimes.com/2008/01/28/business/media/28target.html
5   http://news.bbc.co.uk/2/hi/uk_news/education/6970570.stm
6   www.adweek.com/digital/brandjacking-how-to-prevent-trolls-and-other-internet-pirates-from-harming-your-brand/
7   https://www.theguardian.com/media/2006/oct/17/marketingandpr.newmedia
8   I was one of the co-founders of the United Kingdom's first social media for business conference, Blogging4Business, back in 2006.
9   www.theguardian.com/news/blog/2009/jul/23/youtube-united-breaks-guitars-video
10 My consultancy was working with Lloyds Banking Group at the time and alerted the bank about the existence of the video.
11 Bernhard Warner and Matthew Yeomans (2012). *#FAIL: The 50 Greatest Social Media Screw-Ups*. SMI Publishing.
12 www.theguardian.com/sustainable-business/nestle-facebook
13 www.wired.com/2006/12/tahoe/
14 Bernhard Warner and Matthew Yeomans (2012). *#FAIL: The 50 Greatest Social Media Screw-Ups*. SMI Publishing.
15 www.newyorker.com/business/currency/jpmorgans-twitter-mistake
16 https://www.newyorker.com/business/currency/jpmorgans-twitter-mistake
17 www.nytimes.com/2017/04/10/business/united-flight-passenger-dragged.html
18 www.washingtonpost.com/news/dr-gridlock/wp/2017/04/27/united-dragging-report-our-review-shows-that-many-things-went-wrong-that-day
19 www.theguardian.com/business/2017/may/02/united-airlines-ceo-oscar-munoz-house-committee
20 https://thelede.blogs.nytimes.com/2007/02/16/held-hostage-on-the-tarmac-time-for-a-passenger-bill-of-rights/
21 Warner and Yeomans, *#FAIL: The 50 Greatest Social Media Screw-Ups*.

Part 2

The trust factors

Chapter 4

Collaboration and the power of the crowd

In January 2013, Verizon CEO Lowell McAdam took the stage at the annual Consumer Electronics Show in Las Vegas to herald his company's bold, new sustainability initiative: a multi-year innovation project called Powerful Answers.

The project was created to raise awareness for the wireless network's new 4G service and its centrepiece was a $10 million crowdsourced challenge for entrepreneurs, individuals and companies to generate new ideas in the health care, education and sustainability sectors. "We know that to move this industry forward, the whole ecosystem needs to be involved in the innovation process," explained McAdam.[1]

Verizon's big idea wasn't exactly new. In fact it was just the latest in a series of innovation marketing campaigns that sought to embrace crowdsourcing. For the past three years companies like General Electric (GE), PepsiCo, Sony, Kimberly-Clark, Marks & Spencer and Heineken had been running similar sustainability collaboration and awareness raising competitions and campaigns. All of these "powerful ideas" either used social networks to inspire consumer collaboration around sustainable action or they embraced crowdsourcing as a mobilising tool to tap into the so-called wisdom of the crowd and demonstrate the importance of community in decision-making.

"Customer centric" is a powerful new mantra within modern corporations. It's not hard to see why. Customers/consumers have never wielded more online power than they do in the social media age. At the same time, companies continually find themselves depicted in the media and social media as unethical, inauthentic and, sometimes, downright criminal. For many CEOs, there is a sense that the common bond between company and customer has been lost. Collaborating with the public on sustainability projects and issues using crowdsourcing and crowdfunding is one possible way of regaining trust and respect.

The potential of social media technologies to transform online collaboration and community action had been apparent for nearly a decade before the idea of crowdsourcing gained traction. In 1999, as documented in Chapter 1, the *Cluetrain Manifesto* foresaw how social media communication would create more customer-sensitive brands and companies. Then in 2004, *New Yorker* writer James Surowiecki penned *The Wisdom of Crowds,* an influential book that examined how group decision-making is often better than individual expertise. It was a powerful idea and one reinforced by journalist Dan Gillmor, who in his book of the same year titled, *We The Media,* described how, in the new social media age: "My readers know more than I do."

The common theme running through all this smart thinking was that social media sites and technologies had created platforms for crowd-based collaboration on a scale unthinkable just a few years before. However, it took a *Wired* magazine writer, Jeff Howe, to document how this collaborative action mentality was being shaped into a business process. In a 2006 article, Howe coined the term "crowdsourcing", which he defined in this way:

> Crowdsourcing represents the act of a company or institution taking a function once performed by employees and outsourcing it to an undefined (and generally large) network of people in the form of an open call. This can take the form of peer-production (when the job is performed collaboratively), but is also often undertaken by sole individuals. The crucial prerequisite is the use of the open call format and the large network of potential laborers.[2]

For many brands, however, the initial appeal of crowdsourcing was less about internal business transformation and collaboration and more about finding a cool new way to "join the conversation," to quote the cliché of the time. It was, after all, the first years of social media marketing, and most savvy brands were fixated on the persuasive power of user-generated content and referrals from friends – the so-called Referral Economy. What could be more compelling and persuasive than crowdsourcing love for your brand?

It would be very easy to criticise the early crowdsourcing experiments undertaken by brands. Many, after all, made plenty of mistakes, as documented in Chapter 3. Yet, at the same time, it's hard to think of another era when so many companies were prepared to ask their own communities for help in creating better business ideas or helping society.

The Pepsi Refresh Project was the first major crowdsourced social responsibility project, and it made other companies sit up and take notice. In early 2010, PepsiCo announced it would forego its Superbowl advertising spend for something very different. With the United States still reeling from the global financial crisis, PepsiCo pledged to donate to worthy community projects 1 million dollars each month for one year. The projects would be crowdsourced via a social media platform and each applicant – be it a local charity, community group or educational interest – would use its own social networks to raise support for its projects. The projects that got the most votes on the Pepsi Refresh Project platform in any given month would win the million-dollar prize.

The Pepsi Refresh Project called on people throughout the United States to nominate and vote on community projects that sought to bring about positive social change. PepsiCo pledged to donate the $20 million it normally spent on the Super Bowl to fund the winning entries. PepsiCo had a dedicated Refresh website but it mobilised the campaign using Facebook and Twitter. The response was enormous. The site attracted more than 2.5 million visitors when voting went live in February 2010 and generated media coverage in the form of 1,600 blog posts, 170,000 tweets and 1,300 online news stories. Ultimately some 61 million votes were cast for the various projects.[3]

The Pepsi Refresh Project shook up the world of corporate and social responsibility not because of the amount of money being donated but because of the way PepsiCo was doing it. Dumping the Superbowl was a big deal. Adopting a creative consumer marketing approach to supporting good causes was an even bigger deal. While some observers at the time complained that Pepsi Refresh was mainly about helping PepsiCo's bottom line (it didn't, as later figures would prove)[4] the soft-drink maker's commitment-to-community credentials soared, despite the growing health questions about the amount of sugar used in its core product.

If Pepsi Refresh ultimately was little more than a socially charged piece of cause marketing, GE's Ecomagination Challenge, also launched in 2010, was something quite different. Like PepsiCo, GE pledged to give away millions of dollars by setting a crowdsourced challenge. However, its challenge was geared to the company's business objective of developing clean energy. The smartest clean energy ideas would not only be rewarded with cash to invest but would also gain from GE mentoring.

Back in 2005, GE CEO Jeffrey Immelt had created a new corporate initiative called Ecomagination to develop new, sustainable, power grid (and off grid) technologies – a market estimated to be worth hundreds of billions of dollars over the coming decades. To help jump-start the project, GE partnered with Silicon Valley venture capital firms to help source and fund the brightest minds in sustainable energy. But GE needed to cast a wider net if Ecomagination was to be a success. That's when it decided to set the Ecomagination Challenge – GE would commit $200 million to help entrepreneurs bring their sustainable energy ideas to market and it would award $100,000 in prize money to the winners. GE partnered with crowdsourcing platform, Brightidea, to run the Ecomagination Challenge – over 10 weeks it generated more than 3,500 submissions, 80,000 comments and 120,000 votes. Twelve winners were selected to be funded and receive mentoring from GE.

The GE Ecomagination Challenge (which ran annually for another three years) showed how a company could use social media thinking both to promote and further its own sustainability goals and credentials. As the company itself described the project, Ecomagination Challenge was an "efficient magnet, attracting so many good ideas that GE has been able to enter into commercial partnerships with 22 start-ups representing a broad spectrum of technologies".[5] In 2011, GE also created the Healthyimagination challenge to crowdsource ideas around early breast cancer detection and diagnosis.

Soon other companies, like Kimberly-Clark, were embracing GE's model with projects such as Huggie's Mom's Inspired where entrepreneurial mothers were encouraged to submit new business ideas for funding and business mentoring from the company. The winners would get their ideas funded and brought to market while Kimberly-Clark would own the intellectual property for the ideas it funded. Even the oil and gas sector engaged the public. In 2015 Norwegian oil company Statoil (in partnership with GE) created its own crowdsourcing innovation challenge, reaching out to experts, academics and innovators to develop sustainable approaches to reduce the environmental impacts of using sand in shale oil drilling.[6]

Of course, for every crowdsourced competition that augmented a company's real sustainability activities there were any number of more fluffy campaigns that made a company look good but achieved little else. Yet the evident enthusiasm of the online public to join with companies and work on projects for a communal greater good – and one that made shrewd business sense – clearly resonated with a cadre of mid-level and newly senior business executives who began to grasp how crowdsourced ideas and actions could deliver real value to their businesses, and not just through marketing and good public relations.

Companies like Starbucks and Dell came to realise that the wisdom of the crowd could also have a positive effect connecting customer relations to business planning and research and development. Both MyStarbucksIdea and Dell's IdeaStorm, though hardly perfect models of crowdsourced action, pointed to what was possible in terms of better business when companies opened up about the challenges they faced and sought advice from parts of the community they maybe would never have thought to consult in the past.

Marks & Spencer mobilised the crowd for a different purpose through Shwopping – a consumer behaviour-change programme that used a range of collaborative tools including social networks and gamification to inspire consumers to reduce the amount of clothes being sent to landfill in the United Kingdom. (See the Q&A at the end of the chapter.)

Perhaps one of the most exciting fields for sustainable crowdsourcing success came from health care and life sciences. One pharmaceutical company, Transparent Life Sciences, grew its business by using crowdsourced open innovation in drug research to develop promising drug compounds and design studies. At the University of Washington, scientists took crowdsourced research one step further by building a game interface to gain insight and conduct research about protein structure analysis and design. The Fold. it platform helped scientific researchers play video games to fold the best proteins and, in turn, contribute to medical science breakthroughs. The protein folding game also helped Carnegie Mellon make significant breakthroughs in understanding the structure of the AIDS virus.

Looking to the crowd for funding

Funding has long been one of the biggest barriers to bringing smart new ideas to life. If you're an entrepreneur, getting people to buy into your great idea is one thing. Getting them to actually invest money into the project is quite another. That was especially true in the wake of the 2008 financial crash as banks became risk averse and funds for clean tech, environmental and sustainability projects dried up.

That's why crowdfunding, an offshoot of the crowdsourcing philosophy, captured the imagination of so many companies, young and old. By asking "the crowd" to judge the value of start-up business and creative visions, entrepreneurs put their faith in a peer-to-peer funding model that promises transparency and a sense of community for both funder and fundees.

The poster child and first mover for this movement was Kickstarter. Through this online bidding site, a host of entrepreneurs, artists and other groups with big ideas but small budgets polished their business plans and online elevator pitches in the hope that the Kickstarter community would pony up enough funds to get their ventures started.

Kickstarter became a success because it spotted a big gap in the new disruptive creative industries market. The explosion of online and social media challenged the traditional business models of the music, film and publishing industries. In turn, and counterproductively, those industries became even more risk-averse – putting their faith in supposed guaranteed blockbusters rather than investing and nurturing innovative artists and performers.

Kickstarter provided a model for that innovation and creativity to flourish – its success based in no small part on its "all or nothing" rules to funding. If a project's stated funding goal wasn't met in the time given to raise the money then none of the prospective funders are charged and the project doesn't receive any funds. This made entrepreneurs and creative groups think twice about asking for too much funding and protected (to a certain extent) the funders from throwing money at projects that will never come to fruition.

But the all or nothing model of funding wasn't perfect for all types of research projects, especially if the research was being undertaken for say a medical research, biotech or green tech project that is still years away from becoming a marketable product. Other more niche platforms like Funda-Geek – aimed at crowdfunding technology and scientific projects at universities and research institutions – offered both all or nothing funding for commercial ventures and partial, incremental funding for non-profit oriented research projects.

The Kickstarter revolution showed the sustainability community an alternative path to fund innovation. Around 2013, along with FundaGeek, crowdfunding sites like RocketHub and MedStartr started to provide bespoke crowdfunding support for life science and medical research ventures – areas not covered by Kickstarter.

RocketHub offered a lot of the same opportunities as Kickstarter but with a strong science bent. It helped crowdfund projects with titles like, "Do tiny microbes in the soil help marine trees get established?" and "Changing the face of farming." RocketHub also offered a "Launchpad" for new promising ventures that were voted up or down a funding ladder by a combination of the RocketHub executive team, the site's Facebook community and a rotating group of guest judges.

MedStartr, a crowdfunding site for medical innovation, covered areas such as infectious disease, rheumatoid arthritis and breast cancer. It was started to offer a platform for the many stakeholders – patients, friends and family; medical professionals, researchers and entrepreneurs – who want to drive innovation, disruption and new breakthroughs in the health care space.

MedStartr and other new social sites dedicated to health, medicine and pharmaceuticals will always need to navigate the strict regulations established to protect patients. Yet, in time these news ventures could pioneer new medical devices, new research areas of expertise, drug development or even infrastructure needs for hospitals and clinics.

That's the sort of disruptive power that makes big companies sit up and pay attention. Spanish bank BBVA, for example, incorporated crowdfunding into its Friends and Family microlending platform for Spanish communities.

Crowdsourcing a crisis response

Sometimes it takes a real crisis to open the eyes of both governments and companies to the need for change. Hurricane Sandy, and the devastation it brought to New York in 2012, will likely go down in history as the moment local authorities and corporations in the United States really understood the cost to society and business of climate change. And, as the response to Sandy demonstrated, if cities are going to prepare and plan sustainable societies that can handle the future coming storms, harnessing the combined power of social media, crowdsourcing and Big Data analysis will be crucial.

Social media has proved very adept at covering disasters. Media coverage of the July 7, 2005 London bombings was notable for the way journalists used citizen mobile phone footage and social media commentary to help tell a fast-moving and very confusing story. Since then, whenever a disaster occurs you can be sure someone will be close by, camera phone and connected social network account at the ready, to provide breaking news footage.

Because of this broadcast phenomenon we now know exactly what it looks like to be swept up in a tsunami, escape a terrorist attack, live through an earthquake and even be part of an emergency plane crash landing on New York's Hudson River. Indeed, the knowledge that everyday folk are likely to capture dramatic news moments has prompted major media organisations like the BBC to search for social media viewpoints for most of their breaking news stories. CNN went one better when it set up an entire division on its website devoted to citizen journalism called iReport.

So, as Hurricane Sandy caused havoc across New York City, Long Island and the New Jersey shore, it was natural that people turned to Twitter, Facebook and YouTube to post and share their images and reflections of the super storm. They were aided in their understanding of Sandy by new crisis-mapping tools.

During the 2011 Japan earthquake and tsunami, as well as during New Zealand's Christchurch earthquake of 2010, crowdsourced, crisis-mapping sites provided by the likes of Ushahidi and Google Maps played an important role in helping local people and organisations identify communities that were crying out for relief. The two organisations were in action again during Sandy, providing platforms for people around the Tri-State area to map the flood fallout and helping news organisations like Huffington Post cover the crisis.[7] Other local people made use of another mapping site, Mappler, to create an up-to-the minute map of open gas stations.[8]

With the established civic infrastructure in disarray, people turned to social media sites and tools to connect, share and collaborate on core needs – and the authorities themselves wasted no time using social media to show how hard they were working on the clean-up. The Metropolitan Transit Authority (MTA) posted hundreds of photos on its Flickr account[9] demonstrating how its workers were pumping out flooded tunnels and repairing mile upon mile of damaged subway tracks. The Federal Emergency Management Agency (FEMA), for its own part, ran a monitoring service of all rumours circulating on social media during the crisis and then used that information to publish a "rumour control" blog countering damaging misinformation.

All told, it would take a small army of crisis analysts and researchers to sift through and make sense of all the Sandy-related content created and information shared through social media. But that's exactly the project New York and New Jersey will have to undertake as those states make plans for future flood and hurricane protection.

Too often we look at social media as an ephemeral medium. It's fast and noisy but also quite disposable in many ways. Yet from a research, data-crunching or mapping point of view, the social media "story" of Hurricane Sandy offered a treasure trove of information that can help prepare for future storms. For years climate scientists and weather researchers had been projecting what could happen to New York City if it was hit by a super storm. Now, in the wake of the realisation that the worst had happened, authorities found themselves with a rich mix of scientific and emergency services data combined with millions of first-hand social media accounts as well as crowdsourced maps of what went wrong and what went right during the storm.

Establishing a collaborative, forward-thinking approach to learning from and using social media in a crisis isn't just important for New York's Tri-State region. It's likely to be relevant for most major urban areas all over the world. By 2050 nearly 75 percent of the world's population will be living in cities. Most of those cities sit near the coast or on major lakes and rivers. But in an age of ever-increasing extreme weather patterns, notably super storms, living so close to water becomes as much a liability as an aesthetic pleasure.

Cities all over the world are at risk from extreme weather conditions and other infrastructure crises. That's one reason why, in recent years, a number of companies like Philips, Siemens and IDEO,[10] along with NGOs and groups like the C40 Cities,[11] have created dedicated research projects aimed at using crowdsourcing to plan the future of sustainable cities. In one United Nations–funded project, researchers in Bangkok used a crowdsourcing mobile app to get local people to conduct real-time flood monitoring.

One of the most advanced approaches to tapping the wisdom of the crowd to tackle city infrastructure breakdown came in the shape of IBM's Smarter Cities business programme. It combined crowdsourced conversations and Big Data computing to create a new way of seeing and analysing complex urban logistical issues.

In Rio de Janeiro, IBM Smarter Cities worked with local authorities to create a new automated alert system[12] that notified city officials and emergency personnel when changes occurred in the flood and landslide forecast for the city of Rio de Janeiro. IBM's system used algorithms to predict how much rain would fall in a given square kilometre and harnessed social media chatter to add value to the data. The company estimated the system could drastically reduce the reaction times to emergency situations by using instantaneous mobile communications, including automated email notifications and instant messaging, to reach emergency personnel and local people.

IBM, through its Social Business unit, could analyse social media conversations and use social technologies to create more effective business operations. Combine this expertise with the Big Data crunching capabilities that made Smarter Cities a success and you start to see how all that online chatter around disasters like Hurricane Sandy might offer valuable insight for building better, more sustainable cities.

IBM also made digital collaboration mainstream through its "Jam" events and open innovation platform, an online service to help crowdsourced communities brainstorm ideas and specific challenges. In the United Kingdom, IBM worked with the Prince of Wales Trust and nine major brands to create a Jam around sustainable living and business. In a similar vein UK retailer Sainsbury's crowdsourced ideas from a pool of 155 companies – including rivals Tesco and Marks & Spencer – to help improve the retailer's sustainability marketing.

Unilever, for its part, created an Open Innovation submission platform[13] operated by collaboration platform, Yet2, where it invited outside potential partners to help meets its list of sustainability "WANTS".[14] Unilever's main rival, Procter & Gamble (P&G), meanwhile, developed its own open innovation-sourcing site called Connect + Develop.[15]

It was in the spirit of an IBM Jam that Unilever undertook a real crowdsourced experiment in 2012. The Sustainable Living Lab was a one-day collaboration platform to help the company prioritise and coordinate sustainability targets.[16] Some 2,200 sustainability leaders and experts from 77 countries took part in the 24-hour online "big think" about four key issues: sustainable sourcing; sustainable production and distribution; consumer behaviour change; and recycling and waste. The key to productive discussion and planning came in the curation of the event. It was invitation only and 80 external experts along with 100 Unilever managers from R&D, procurement, marketing and customer development took part in curating the crowd. The conclusions of the Lab were shared with the participants and put on the action agenda of the Unilever Sustainable Living Plan Steering Team, comprising senior managers from Unilever's Leadership Executive.

The sharing economy?

When Airbnb, Lyft and Uber burst on the scene a few years ago the business world was abuzz with the potential for a new "sharing economy".

Advocates explained how these services would provide people with new ways of making money by utilising their homes and vehicles to their full potential, while offering a service that could save energy, reduce waste and bring communities together by sharing their resources and time.

Today more than 100 companies are considered part of this industry built on digitally enabled collaboration. They range from the well-known urban transportation and accommodation services to start-up communities specialising in tools and toy sharing. Even big corporates like Marriott, Walgreens and Avis have got into the sharing economy game.

Yet, as the sector has developed the sustainability utopia of the sharing economy has come into question. Both Airbnb and Uber (especially Uber) have had to counter numerous claims that their services don't protect the well-being of the workers who use their platforms. Uber, Lyft and other sharing economy transportation companies also face environmental concerns over whether the service they provide actually reduces the number of cars on the road, or adds to the congestion by encouraging more people to drive for a living. Then there is the larger issue of whether companies that have few employees but depend on a great deal of freelance labour can really be sustainable for society. Throughout the world governments and regulators continue to fight with so-called gig economy companies about whether the people getting work through their app-driven platforms are really just freelance contractors or whether they should be considered employees – with the same associated vacation pay, pensions and taxes.

The sharing economy takes many forms, however, and shouldn't simply be judged by the bullying business culture practiced by a few greedy companies. Many sharing platforms and services operate on a micro or community level, or are geared to a specific sector or service. Take Streetbank, a social network built on the philosophy of neighbourly collaboration that helps members share anything from borrowing a drill to donating an unwanted food mixer to lending your step ladder, or even organising a get together to help clear an older neighbour's backyard. Streetbank provides a platform to share information about local events, and it has the status of a charity, which makes it eligible for grant funding, as well as receiving donations from members. Since it launched in 2010, more than 60,000 people have shared more than £1.5 million worth of items and skills using Streetbank.

Other major companies have also embraced sharing philosophies. Workspace on Demand is a collaboration established in 2013 between Marriott Hotels and sharing workspace start-up, LiquidSpace. Marriott freed up a number of spaces within its US hotel chain that would otherwise remain unused, and LiquidSpace brokered those spaces through its online platform and community. The upshot was a more efficient use of Marriott's dead office space and, moving forward, a potentially lucrative new line of business for other hotels around the world to tap into.

In 2014, a drugstore chain, Walgreens, and TaskRabbit, an errand-outsourcing start-up, collaborated to provide a localised solution to the common cold. The collaboration enabled improved remote health care, but also more localised economic opportunities for low-skilled workers. People who live in one of 19 US cities serviced by TaskRabbit were able to use its iPhone app to get cold remedies from Walgreens delivered directly to their door. The under-the-weather user would post what they needed and one of TaskRabbit's local members would take the job, collect the cold medicine from Walgreens and deliver it. (In 2017 TaskRabbit was acquired by Ikea.)

As companies confront many of the challenges posed by greater urbanisation, resource scarcity and a changing consumer culture, they will need to collaborate with the public and local communities more than ever before, whether it's through crowdsourcing, crowdfunding or sharing-economy models. In doing so they will find that working together can break down many of the barriers that the corporate world has put up between itself and the public over the years. But, if those companies want to really win the public's trust, not only must their collaboration and partnership be authentic – as demonstrated through useful services and feedback – but it must also be undertaken with a commitment to radical transparency.

Q&A with Adam Elman, former head of global delivery for Plan A at Marks & Spencer

From 2010 to 2017 Adam Elman was responsible for driving and reporting on the delivery of Plan A across every part of the business, including Shwopping, the breakthrough consumer collaboration campaign.

Q: How did Shwopping come about?

A: Shwopping has been through many versions. When M&S [Marks & Spencer] was setting Plan A back in 2007 it was designed to tackle big issues. One of those was clothes going to landfill – about 10,000 items of clothing every five minutes. Clearly as the biggest clothing retailer in the United Kingdom that something that we had to deal with.

At the time we didn't know how to do this. While M&S had plenty of expertise in designing, manufacturing and selling garments, clearly we weren't experts in collecting garments and giving them a second life. When we looked at who were experts the number one player was Oxfam. We came up an innovative partnership where we would encourage our customers to take their old M&S clothes to Oxfam. They were a perfect partner because they knew how to deal with the garments – they could either resell them in their stores or they had ethical routes to send them overseas or routes in place to recycle when the garments weren't wearable. Also they had a presence on every high street.

That was the original programme called the "clothes exchange" and it worked really well – there were lots of donations for Oxfam – and customers loved it.

A few years later we thought, how could we move this forward? Some of the customer feedback we'd received asked how could we expand it for all garments, not just ones sold by M&S. And while Oxfam shops were in many locations we also wanted to make it even easier for people to donate. So the concept we came up with was we'd invite customers on one particular day to bring their garments into M&S stores and we'd pass them onto Oxfam. This was the one-day wardrobe clear-out. We ran it several times and each time we had some 400,000 garments worth hundreds of thousands of pounds for Oxfam.

This is what gave us the inspiration for Shwopping. Rather than make it a one-day event we said we'll offer this service every day. The motivation was: if you're coming to buy something, why not drop something off that you don't need? We'll pass it on to Oxfam to give it a second life and help raise funds to fight poverty.

Q: What were the main challenges you faced with a programme like Shwopping?

A: One of our initial challenges was when I first explained the concept of the one-day wardrobe clear-out to our retail director the reaction was "you're having a laugh!" After all, we run these beautiful stores and we spend a great deal of time and money making them fantastic and you're suddenly saying you want our customers to bring back their old unwanted garments? There were other very valid concerns. What quantity of clothes was going to come back? Where is it all going to go? How are we going to operationally manage this? Could we manage this from a health and safety and security point of view?

This was something we (and no-one else) had ever done before. Our ambition was very high but we had to test and trial and learn to see what works for customers, what works from a logistical point of view. For example, it only worked if we could transport the clothes to Oxfam on the back of empty vehicles delivering to the stores. If we'd had to put on more vehicles then that would have been a carbon problem. We didn't want to fix one issue while causing another issue.

Q: Did running Shwopping give M&S insight into managing other sustainability initiatives at scale?

A: It's something we think about in everything we do. We have to take a balanced and informed view to make sure we do the right thing. That's also why we work with external partners and governments to tap into their expertise.

Sometimes as a business we just have to make choices. When we decided to charge for plastic carrier bags in the United Kingdom it was hugely popular with some people and hugely unpopular with other people. Now though, 10 years on in the United Kingdom, everyone pays for carrier bags and that's partly because M&S made that bold decision back then. Sometimes we do just have to jump into the unknown but as a rule we work with experts internal and external to make sure we've got as much insight, science and knowledge as possible.

Q: One interesting part about Shwopping was that you were reusing clothes to make new clothes. How appealing was that to consumers?

A: It was less about consumers to begin with and more about a genuine business benefit by making our supply chains more resilient. We know obtaining raw materials at the quality and quantity and the pricing we want is going to be increasingly difficult based on the environmental and social issues the industry faces. The opportunity to have large streams of fibre coming back that we could reuse clearly made a lot of sense. It was also a great opportunity to turn it into a consumer proposition but we had to be really careful – second-hand fibre doesn't necessarily sound that attractive so the branding and marketing around the idea needed a lot of thought.

We did release a number of products that sold well and we had a great story to tell around it but the reality is that this isn't an area that has progressed at the pace we would have liked – mainly because of a technology reason. Reusing fibre works very well at a high end – cashmere for instance – but at the low end there aren't the solutions yet to scale up reused fibres either because of cost or technology and the issues with mixed fibres. M&S like many others are investing a lot of time and money to find those solutions.

Q: What effect did Shwopping have on employees? Did it help them embrace Plan A?

A: It had multiple benefits. Sometimes sustainability is hard to get your head around but this was something that was very customer facing and it was driving people into the stores so they could see not just the environmental but also the commercial benefit. It was something they could get involved in. It was something very real and they could see the impact – the mountains of clothes building up. They also got great feedback from the Oxfam stores so it was very real.

Q: And did it resonate with the community?

A: It worked on many levels but there are lots of things we do in sustainability that never touch all of our people because they are managed centrally or aren't seen visually by staff. This was something that was very visual and covered issues of fashion, waste and poverty. What's interesting is that different people get excited about different parts of Shwopping. Some might be excited by the environmental side of it while others are more interested that we're working with Oxfam to fight poverty.

Q: What turned an interesting but small-scale sustainability initiative into a campaign that caught the national mood?

A: When we launched Shwopping as a campaign we really took the clothes exchange to the next phase. We did a big launch where we took over Brick Lane (heart of London's garment district) and covered it in 10,000 items of garments to visualise the issue and bring it to life. It was covered globally by the media. In truth it's a big challenge to get people to bring back garments – it's not like shaking a bucket in front of someone and asking them to donate a bit of spare change. You've got to go into your wardrobe, find the garments you don't want, put them in a bag and bring them to our stores. It's a big ask.

Clearly our goal was, how do we change consumer behaviour? How do we make recycling clothes in our stores normal? Although over 27 million garments have been donated, in truth we have not achieved as much progress as we would like.

Q: What about the social media effect? You had a Facebook campaign, gamification and a dedicated app. Did it help?

A: Yes, we did a lot in terms of Twitter campaigns and gamification. To be honest a lot of it didn't work just because the nature of M&S's business and the type of consumer we have. We have a generally older consumer and actually the reality of using social media and logging into the app when you're wandering around the store with your used clothes in your bag wasn't really that practical. A lot of people used the app but it was a dedicated few rather than the masses.

However it was important to try these things – some worked and some didn't. What really did work for us was the storytelling around Shwopping. We did a documentary video with Joanna Lumley, who went to Senegal to visit a social enterprise set up by Oxfam, to discover the full story of what happens to the garments. The video went out on our social media channels and got a great deal of shares and retweets. The storytelling is important because people want to see the positive outcome of their actions.

Q: Looking back, what was biggest lesson you learned for sustainability communication?

A: You need to continually revisit and push on adding new levels of interaction. We keep growing it, then it plateaus and so we think about how do we take it to the next level. It's also really important to remember and revisit why we started this project in the first place, and that was to reduce the amount of clothes going to landfill. Nowadays when you looked at the sector there are lots of brands who have clothes recycling schemes. Sometimes people say: are you not upset about this – competitors copying your idea? On the contrary, this campaign was about behaviour change and we'll never change consumers if it's just M&S doing this type of work. Fundamentally we were trying to tackle an issue and the more companies we have working on this the better.

Notes

1 https://techcrunch.com/2013/01/08/verizon-powerful-answers-awards/
2 http://crowdsourcing.typepad.com/cs/2006/06/crowdsourcing_a.html
3 http://adage.com/article/digital/marketing-pepsi-refresh-case-marketing-textbooks/141973/
4 http://adage.com/article/viewpoint/a-teaching-moment-professors-evaluate-pepsi-refresh-project/237629/
5 https://books.google.co.uk/books?id=KBd-Tl4vfNEC&pg=PT19&dq=ge+ecomaginatio n+challenge+2010&hl=en&sa=X&ved=0ahUKEwjF05T0t5LVAhXIKsAKHRL4Bw0Q6 AEIKDAA#v=onepage&q=ge%20ecomagination%20challenge%202010&f=false
6 www.statoil.com/en/news/archive/2015/07/21/21JulInnovationwinners.html
7 http://blog.ushahidi.com/index.php/2012/10/29/hurricane-sandy-in-maps/
8 http://mappler.net/gasstation/
9 www.flickr.com/photos/mtaphotos/
10 www.challengedetroit.org/
11 http://live.c40cities.org/
12 www.nytimes.com/2012/03/04/business/ibm-takes-smarter-cities-concept-to-rio-de-janeiro.html
13 https://oiportal.yet2.com/
14 http://yet2.com/
15 http://pgconnectdevelop.inovasuite.com/pg/login.do?method=challengeLogin&challe nge_id=307
16 www.unilever.com/sustainable-living/sustainabilityevents/index.aspx

Chapter 5

Radical transparency

The smartphone, and our access to instant information, is already transforming the purchasing decisions of consumers. Today, shoppers are comparing prices and consumer reviews of goods on their phones while shopping in store; they are checking on the sustainability values of seafood and other produce via dedicated apps; and, as we saw in Chapter 2, their opinions of brands are being influenced by activism awareness–raising campaigns delivered direct via social media.

That trend is likely to increase as more young people come to expect transparency and higher ethical standards from the companies whose products they buy. Numerous studies of that supposedly all-important Millennial demographic suggest that young people want more sustainable products, services and experiences – and they want companies to back up their sustainability claims with evidence of action.[1]

For example, in 2013, following the Rana Plaza factory disaster, two young fashion designers – Carry Somers and Orsola de Castro – founded Fashion Revolution, a social media movement designed to demand transparency from the apparel industry. In 2016, its hashtag campaign #whomademyclothes was shared by more than 70,000 social media users and reached the conversation streams of an estimated 150 million people – an enormous awareness-raising campaign that prompted hundreds of brands, including Boden, American Apparel, Massimo Dutti, Fat Face and Zara, to respond about their sustainable working commitments. In addition, more than 2,600 producers, garment workers and makers used Instagram and Twitter to tell the world #imadeyourclothes, and share their stories of working conditions.[2] Other apparel companies like online retailer Everlane have put transparency in sourcing, supply chain costs and pricing at the heart of their offering.[3]

Technology is offering new opportunities for demonstrating transparency. In 2017, Avery Dennison, one of the world's largest apparel and footwear labelling companies, partnered with Evrythng, an Internet of Things start-up, to produce a new generation of Net-connected labels that could allow consumers to check the authenticity or manufacturing history of products, including information on sourcing and ingredients as well as options for recycling them in the future.[4]

Krug Champagne is another company that realises it must show transparency to win more consumers. It developed a digital tracking system that allows consumers to learn the environmental and social history of each champagne bottle it sells. Organic Valley is taking a more hands-on approach to demonstrating transparency. It created a website that not only informs consumers about the farming conditions of its dairy suppliers but also arranges trips for consumers to visit the farms and judge the quality for themselves.[5]

Increasingly, authenticity is "the biggest key for consumers. They want to know who's creating their food. Consumers want to trust the suppliers of their food," Sarah Z. Masoni, from the Food Innovation Center at Oregon State University, explained to *The New York Times* in a 2017 story about changing consumer tastes in food.[6]

Despite all the evidence demonstrating the evolving and heightened expectations of consumers, many companies still find it hard to be transparent in their business practices – often due to a combination of factors including an insular corporate culture, convoluted and overly complex working practices and contractor relationships, an overly defensive legal strategy and a communication framework aimed at protecting reputation at the expense of building relationships.

It's no wonder then that brands tend to embrace greater transparency only after coming under attack by consumers, the media, regulators and activists – often feeding off each other.

In 2012 McDonald's faced exactly this scenario. After decades as the undisputed king of fast food, the company found itself challenged by a new generation of consumers whose tastes and standards were changing, and who increasingly placed a premium on the quality of the food they ordered rather than how swiftly it was served up.

Consumer concerns had been stoked during the previous decade by investigative books like *Fast Food Nation* and agitprop documentaries like *Supersize Me* and *Food Inc.,* which had raised disturbing questions about the ingredients and welfare of the animals used to make fast food, and for McDonald's in particular. Who wouldn't be shocked to hear that their burger and fries contained petroleum or that some iconic Big Macs contained "pink slime" – beef scraps turned into a paste that had been treated with ammonia?[7]

Not surprisingly these stories resonated and lingered with the newly connected consumer, who wasted no time sharing the horror stories about food quality with friends. On Twitter and other social platforms, McDonald's was portrayed as the public enemy of healthy eating and lambasted for luring children over to the dark side of fast food through Happy Meal toys.

McDonald's was still serving 28 million customers each day but, as the dramatic growth of so-called healthy fast-food companies such as Chipotle and Panera Bread demonstrated, the company knew it had a fight on its hands to hold on to market share in the future. McDonald's had already invested in a makeover of its restaurants and was working to offer healthier menu options to meet those changing consumer tastes. Yet it still faced a massive reputation issue.

McDonald's first steps in the rehabilitation of its image on social media came in 2010 when it invited a group of Mommy Bloggers to its Oak Brook, Illinois, headquarters so they could understand the company's commitment to good food and share the experience with their readers. McDonald's paid some of the blogger's travel expenses but didn't directly compensate them.

Then, in 2012, the company made mainstream an emerging form of food transparency storytelling (some call it "farmer porn") that highlighted real-life working stories of the beef, apple and potato farmers who supply McDonald's.

The US social media and TV campaign #MeettheFarmers featured sun-drenched landscapes, folksy guitar music and happy farmers, of course. The accompanying videos of the farmers were a little contrived but also informative; however, they were soon overshadowed on social media by the chatter around the #McDStories Twitter campaign (see Chapter 3).

In Canada, meanwhile, McDonald's had hit on a far more ambitious way of demonstrating the company's transparency around sourcing and ingredients: it would let consumers ask any questions they want about McDonald's food and the company would answer them in a forthright and honest manner.

Our Food. Your Questions launched in Canada in early 2012. It featured a YouTube video that directed visitors to a dedicated website where they could ask questions about the brand. Visitors identified themselves by logging on through a personal Twitter or Facebook account. Over six months, the McDonald's Canada site received more than 2 million hits and staff answered more than 20,000 questions along the lines of: "Why doesn't your food look like it does in advertising?" and "Is there pink goop in the Chicken McNuggets?"

To make sure it could respond accurately and promptly, McDonald's put together a 10-person response team to answer the queries. The campaign was so successful that it was adapted and embraced by McDonald's operations all over the world and was nominated for a 2016 IPA Effectiveness Award in the United Kingdom because it "demonstrated how to create a bold, comprehensive, well-produced and effective vehicle for transparency".[8]

By the time Our Food. Your Questions reached the United States in 2014, it had added more dynamic transparent storytelling element, including inviting TV news crews behind the scenes to evaluate food processing and enlisting professional sceptic and former *MythBusters* co-host Grant Imahara to film a series of videos debunking those consumer pink slime worries and more.

Consider this post accompanying a video by Imahara on October 15, 2014, on its US Facebook page.

> Fillers. Preservatives. 'Pink Slime.' We've heard the rumors. Ready to hear how we REALLY make our beef patties?

More than 31,000 people "liked" that one post and it was shared through Facebook nearly 17,000 times. It also generated 8,500 comments and McDonald's social media team was on hand to answer many of the indigestible questions being lobbed at them.

Perhaps the most innovative, transparent and, frankly, scary aspect of the US campaign (for the brand at least) was a commitment to answering consumer questions about food quality in real time via social media channels like Facebook and Twitter. In doing so McDonald's was putting its reputation on the line in a way most brands would definitely avoid.

Kevin Newell, executive vice-president chief brand and strategy officer for McDonald's USA, told BurgerBusiness.com (yes, that was a real online publication, though it offered its last bite of industry news in 2016):

> We know some people – both McDonald's fans and skeptics – continue to have questions about our food from the standpoint of the ingredients or how food is prepared at the restaurant. This is our move to ensure we engage people in a two-way dialogue about our food and answer the questions and address their comments. The work we've done in the past has been one-way. We've made nutrition information about our food available for a number of years. But people had to go find it. Now we're inviting consumers to go on a journey with us to get those questions answered.[9]

Interestingly, the McDonald's campaign wasn't entirely new. Back in 2006 the company had trialled a transparency-focused website in the United Kingdom called Make Up Your Own Mind which encouraged customers to ask questions about the brand.[10]

Not everyone was convinced by McDonald's attempts at transparency. *Ad Age* suggested that the McDonald's Canada campaign was actually very tightly managed – it didn't allow users to comment on its YouTube videos, for example. *Time* magazine, meanwhile, warned that transparency alone wouldn't help McDonald's meet the challenge of changing times and tastes: "Millennials are now driving the food bus and they're heading straight to Chipotle and other establishments that are offering healthier options, including foods without genetically engineered or artificial ingredients and meat from animals raised without antibiotics," it wrote.[11]

The problem of overpromising

Chipotle Mexican Grill got its start in Denver back in 1993. By 2010 it was at the vanguard of new group of upstart healthy fast-food brands that had old-school fast-food company executives choking on their fries as the US public began to ask tough questions about the amount of salt, sugar, antibiotics and whatever other chemicals were being pumped into their convenience food.

As *Fast Company* wrote in a 2016 feature story,

> For years, enlightened restaurant-goers, shocked and horrified by *Fast Food Nation*, pink slime, and the evils of Big Food, have felt an almost religious pull to Chipotle's "Food With Integrity" mission – its commitment to fresh ingredients, ethical sourcing, and disrupting the fast-food model – as if eating at a Chipotle could nourish your soul as well as your body.[12]

Chipotle's own research showed that 75 percent of its 800,000 daily customers came for the taste, value and convenience of its food. To further differentiate itself from the fast-food pack, Chipotle decided it "needed to have a general, higher-level message and to tell the story in a more approachable way," Mark Crumpacker, Chipotle's chief marketing officer, told *The New York Times*.[13] The answer was sustainability and Chipotle felt it had a good story to tell. After all, the company was committed to sourcing naturally grown produce and beef, pork and chicken produced without antibiotics.

To inspire customers Chipotle set about extolling sustainable farming in a way the social media–snacking generation would appreciate by commissioning a short animated film, *Back to the Start*. It portrayed a farmer who embraces factory farming before realising the error of his ways and reverts back to sustainable pasture farming.

The film was animated using the same type of stop-motion technique that had made the Wallace and Gromit movies such an international hit, and it featured the Coldplay song, "The Scientist", reimagined by country legend and environmental activist, Willie Nelson.

Back to the Start first aired online in the summer of 2011 accompanied by a YouTube backstory video showing how the film was made – specifically designed to inform and entertain a social media community that had come to expect a "behind the scenes" explanation of the main content. The campaign was a breath of fresh air in a food industry that had been clogged with inane pastiches of happy families and, more recently, overly sincere farmers. More important, it seemed to echo Chipotle's own journey – a conscious departure from factory farming to a more sustainable approach to sourcing. There was even an iTunes download option for the Willie Nelson Coldplay cover with the proceeds going to the Chipotle Cultivate Foundation, which encourages sustainable farming methods and family farming. *Back to the Start* proved so successful online that Chipotle also showed it at 5,700 movie theatres later that year. "People were applauding [in the theatres]," Crumpacker told *Ad Age*, and that, in turn, prompted Chipotle to air the advert on TV during the 2012 Grammy Awards.

The next year Chipotle returned with a new film, *The Scarecrow*, that raised the bar both in terms of creativity and also the tone the company employed to distance itself from other fast-food companies.

The Scarecrow was a lavish animated short film created by Academy-award-winning Moonbot Studios. It was accompanied by an app-based game designed to maximise Chipotle's presence at a time when tablets and mobile phone social media interaction was surging. In the narrative, the Scarecrow is a farmer who finds himself trapped in the industrial agriculture economy. He is shocked to see how chickens and cows are being treated and this experience prompts him to escape the system by growing his own natural produce, so offering a healthy alternative to factory fast food.

As with *Back to the Start*, *The Scarecrow* was accompanied by an inspiring soundtrack – this time an interpretation of *Charlie and the Chocolate Factory*'s "Pure Imagination" sung by Fiona Apple. The effect was mesmerising – *The Scarecrow* pulled at the heartstrings as well as any Hollywood animated kid's movie. Yet, by creating such an aspirational story and by alluding to its superior quality over the McDonald's of the world, Chipotle was setting itself up for a transparency fall.

Journalists, food activists and even the parody web site, Funny or Die, were quick to point out the inconsistencies between the lofty ideals in Chipotle's animated story and the realities of its sourcing. For example, while Chipotle made the film "to highlight issues like the overuse of antibiotics, harsh confinement of animals, the extent to which food is processed,"[14] only about 80 percent of the beef it served was free from antibiotics and growth hormones. The gap wasn't Chipotle's fault, exactly – it sourced as much antibiotic and hormone free beef as the market could produce at the time – but that wasn't a nuance that the agitprop of *The Scarecrow* campaign allowed for.

As the *New Yorker* observed,

> Chipotle falls short of the film's ideals. We can see the Scarecrow's farm for ourselves, but we have to trust Chipotle's assertions that its suppliers meet its standards. The Scarecrow uses only ingredients that conform to his values, but when Chipotle runs out of sustainable beef, a decidedly less happy cow could end up marinated and grilled and nestled beside our cilantro-lime rice.[15]

Ultimately, Chipotle's commitment to transparency had been undermined by its own creativity.

That wasn't the end of the Chipotle transparency saga. In October 2015 the company was hit by an E.coli food poisoning outbreak that affected a number of its restaurants all across the United States. The outbreak lasted months and took a massive financial and reputational toll. In 2016, the company reported a $26.4 million quarterly loss – its first since going public 10 years before. Its stock had plummeted by 30 percent, resulting in shareowner losses of more than $10 billion, and overall sales were down by one-third compared to before the outbreak hit.

In the aftermath of the scandal it became clear that, even though Chipotle was fully committed to sustainable ingredients and sourcing, the size of its operations, the high staff turnover at its restaurants, and the relatively complicated manner of cooking and assembling its freshly made food had all contributed to a breakdown in quality assurance and compliance. In fact, Chipotle had acknowledged as much to investors in its 2013 and 2014 annual reports, writing: "We may be at a higher risk for foodborne-illness outbreaks than some competitors due to our use of fresh produce and meats rather than frozen, and our reliance on employees cooking with traditional methods rather than automation."[16]

Chipotle has been slowly rebuilding its reputation and its market share ever since. Part of the strategy to win back customers was a Summer Rewards Program that offered free food to people making multiple visits to Chipotle between July and September 2016. And to further boost its rehabilitation efforts Chipotle returned to the storytelling theme that had created such a buzz for the brand in the past – namely an online animated short film titled *A Love Story* that also ran in more than 10,000 movie theatres.

The film revisited the recurring conflict that *Back to the Start* and *The Scarecrow* had addressed: how can a company grow big while remaining true to its values? It told the story of two friends and neighbours, a young boy and a young girl who start rival sidewalk juice stands and grow them into fast-food giants only to realise that their dreams and the quality of their offering has been poisoned in the process. Sound familiar?

Certainly media commentators saw an allegoric connection between the storytelling and Chipotle's own corporate journey.

"The film seems to reflect the company's own angst regarding its current state," wrote *Fast Company*, adding:

> The point of *A Love Story*, like two previous award-winning shorts, is that Chipotle is not McDonald's. But it's impossible to ignore a different subtext now given all the change the company has undergone: Is Chipotle in danger of becoming the evil fast-food chain?[17]

Adweek couldn't help but ask:

> Have all these ads actually been a mounting cry for help, which we collectively failed to heed? What will it take for this darling of fast-food chains to . . . return to its first love – fresh food, possibly a future in food trucks?[18]

The credibility gap between Chipotle's creativity and the way it was acting points to a problem all companies (but especially food brands) face in communicating sustainability. There is simply no room for error between what they promise their customers and what they then deliver. Yet at the same time food brands know that they have to keep inspiring their customers and create a vision they will buy into in order to stay relevant in an age where "healthy" and "natural" are the buzzwords for good food.

Who made my clothes?

The year is 1992 and the sports clothing company, Nike, is on the top of its game. Eight years after signalling its intention to dominate the sportswear market by signing a sponsorship deal with basketball superstar, Michael Jordan, the company's sales had topped $3 billion and it had just launched a whole new shopping experience in the form of Niketown.

Then, in August, just as the Barcelona Olympics where Nike featured prominently was taking place, *Harper's* magazine published an expose titled: "The New Free Trade Heel".[19] Its subhead read: "Nike's profits jump on the back of Asian workers" and it outlined the damning working conditions at some of the factories supplying Nike. In one example, an Indonesian worker for a Nike subcontractor was paid just 14 cents an hour.

These weren't the first criticisms of Nike's outsourcing standards. *The Economist* had reported on worker unrest at Nike contractor factories the year before while local Indonesian newspapers had chronicled wage-related protests at some factories as early as 1988 and 1989.

But the *Harper's* story, combined with anti-Nike protests in Barcelona and a CBS interview of Nike factory workers in 1993 guaranteed the sweatshop issue would start to get more mainstream coverage. Then, in 1996, revelations that clothing being produced for TV celebrity Kathie Lee Gifford's designer line was being made by 13- and 14-year-olds working 20-hour days in factories in Honduras turned the issue of sweatshop labour into a national story in the United States.[20]

That year, with questions about its credibility increasing, Nike established a department that would focus on improving the lives of factory workers. Still, though, the negative media coverage of the factories supplying the company increased and the physical protests grew. Star brand ambassador Michael Jordan found himself having to defend Nike's working conditions and a student protest movement across US colleges started to mobilise.

Nike tried to appease critics by commissioning a report into working practices at its contractors' factories but it was widely dismissed as greenwashing. In 1998, as the years of negative publicity hit sales, and as the company was forced to lay off workers, CEO Phil Knight announced Nike would raise the minimum age for workers at its Asian plants and improve factory working conditions.[21] It also pledged to require overseas manufacturers of its products to meet strict US health and safety standards.

"The Nike product has become synonymous with slave wages, forced over-time, and arbitrary abuse," Knight said. "I truly believe the American consumer doesn't want to buy products made under abusive conditions."[22]

Between 2002 and 2004 Nike would perform some 600 factory audits, including return visits to problematic factories as it sought to rectify the serious issues with its sourcing.[23] In 2005 it became the first apparel maker to publish a complete list of factories that it was contracting with and it published a 108-page report revealing conditions and pay in its factories. As the *Guardian* noted at the time, for a company that had spent more than a decade glossing over working conditions, the report

> admits to widespread problems, particularly in Nike's Asian factories. The company said it audited hundreds of factories in 2003 and 2004 and found cases of "abusive treatment", physical and verbal, in more than a quarter of its south Asian plants.[24]

Nike's commitment to improving labour conditions at its contracting factories would continue apace – so much so that, by the time the 2012 Olympics took place, media organisations and NGOs that had been highly critical of Nike started applauding its change in corporate culture even as they urged the company to do more.

"For a company which 20 years ago was denying that workers' rights at supplier factories were any of its concern, Nike has come a long way," *Ethical Consumer* editor Rob Harrison told the *Guardian*.[25]

Within Nike it was clear to the corporate communications and sustainability teams that demonstrating its commitment to transparency was the only way that the company could really shed its lingering sweatshop image. The company was already taking important steps to improve sustainability in other areas. It had been pioneering the use of recycling to produce new products for decades. It was also a founding member of the Sustainable Apparel Coalition,[26] which aims to change the entire system of making clothes. Yet it was still getting beaten up on college campuses for its supply chain labour legacy.

To lift the lid on its operations, Nike launched The Manufacturing Index in 2012.[27] This matrix ranked labour and environmental performance alongside measures of quality, cost and on-time delivery for more than 800 contracted factories that employ 1 million contracted factory workers and 500,000 different products.

The Index included a number of sustainability metrics including water, energy, carbon and waste, as well as health and safety and labour management and integrated performance scoring for quality, cost, delivery and sustainability into a single rating.[28] With each factory awarded a single overall score, the index helped Nike shape a consistent and comprehensive view of its sustainability performance across the world.

To make the Index more accessible still, Nike created an online, searchable global map, showing up-to-date data on every one of the factories where Nike products were made worldwide.

Of course, any pledge of greater transparency naturally attracts greater external scrutiny. Indeed, what makes sustainability so important and yet so hard for all companies is that any achievements have to be maintained over the long term. Let the commitments slip and so does sustainable performance and reputation.

In 2016, *Slate* in conjunction with the Nation Institute published a critical investigation into labour conditions for female workers at Nike contract factories in Vietnam.[29] The story highlighted how Nike's own Code of Conduct was being violated and argued that the experiences of the Vietnamese woman made a mockery of Nike's "Girl Effect" – a charitable initiative started back in 2008 based on the widely held idea that empowering and preparing girls to work is crucial to solving global poverty.

It's clear then, that despite Nike's commitment to greater transparency, the challenges it faces in terms of sustainable supply chains will require constant vigilance.

Looking forward, sustainable innovation will help address some of these problems but, it is unlikely to make the poorly paid workers of South East Asia any better off. As Nike has focused more on suppliers that can meet its growing demands for sustainability improvements, it has reduced the number of contract factories its uses from 785 factories 2013 to 692 at the end of 2015, even as it has increased the volume of products made by 11 percent.[30]

That trend will likely increase in the future. In recent years Nike has pioneered new sustainable methods of manufacturing including 3D printing of shoes and high-tech weaving of fabric to reduce waste and time in production. The upshot of these new breakthrough techniques will result in new decentralised ways of producing clothes and footwear. In fact, it's perfectly conceivable that, one day soon, Nike products could be produced on demand at the same stores where they are sold or at the online delivery hub where they will be dispatched.

"We've set a moonshot challenge to double our business with half the impact," Nike sustainability chief Hannah Jones said in 2016. "It's a bold ambition that's going to take much more than incremental efficiency – it's going to take innovation on a scale we've never seen before."[31]

Intel's conflict minerals of interest

The minerals gold, tantalum, tungsten and tin are vital components in the computers and smartphones we depend on every day.

Sourcing these raw materials is fraught with ethical risk, however. That's because one of the main regions for mining these minerals is the Democratic Republic (DR) of Congo, which, for the past 20 years, has been ravaged by the world's worst conflict since the World War Two. During that time the sale of so-called conflict minerals has directly financed the operations of some of the militias and rogue armies that are responsible for the deaths of an estimated 5.4 million people.[32]

Very few consumers know the problem exists. In the United States for example, only 35 percent of those aged 18 to 35 were aware of conflict minerals, according to a survey commissioned by Intel. But once they understood the importance of the topic, consumers wanted companies to take action, the data showed.[33]

The company, the world's biggest producer of semiconductors, commissioned the survey as part of a strategy raise awareness campaign to accompany cleaning up its own supply chain.

It was in Las Vegas at the 2014 Consumer Electronics Show, the annual over-the-top celebration of all things tech–related, that Intel's CEO Brian Krzanich delivered a keynote address with a difference. Having already unveiled new "smart earbuds", 3D printing devices and better processing power for wearable computing, Krzanich told the attendees:

> Okay. I'm going to switch gears for a minute now. . . . This is not an issue we would normally talk about at CES, but it is an issue that is very important and personal to me. That issue is conflict minerals.[34]

Under the banner of "Conflict-Free", Intel committed to ensure that, from that point on, the materials that go into its products would be sourced responsibly. The company established a consortium of independent, third-party non-profits to work with the local government to audit mines. Once a mine earned a positive rating, its ore would be placed in labelled bags that could be tracked to smelters. Intel also donated $250,000 to a fund to help smelters who want to meet the tech giant's ethical guidelines but couldn't afford to retrace their supply chains.[35]

In addition, Intel became a member of the Conflict-Free Sourcing Initiative, the Global e-Sustainability Initiative and the Public Private Alliance for Responsible Minerals Trade, two industry-based and one cross-sector organisation that promote and help ensure sustainable and conflict-free supply chains.

By 2016, two years after Intel eliminated conflict minerals from all its microprocessors, every Intel product was using minerals from audited mines only. Intel's products featured a "Conflict-Free" product mark to ensure the content of the product were responsibly sourced – enabling more informed consumer decisions.

Unlike some of the major corporate transparency commitments of recent years, Intel wasn't pushed into change by social media agitation, though NGOs had been lobbying tech companies for decades about ethical sourcing standards. The drive for change began a few years before from inside the company, when Krzanich, who previously was in charge of global manufacturing, received a letter from the Enough Project NGO, which specialised in the Congo conflict.[36] External regulations also put pressure on the industry. The 2010 Dodd-Frank Wall Street Reform and Consumer Protection Act required all publicly traded companies to account for conflict minerals.

That prompted a long process of working with (and sometimes putting pressure on) suppliers to improve transparency and ensure conflict minerals didn't enter the supply chain. Yet Intel also understood how a consumer backlash around conflict minerals could damage its reputation. Faced with a ticking reputation time bomb, Intel knew it had to lead, not hide. To raise awareness, Intel created a dedicated website and documentary campaign showing the human and environmental suffering caused by conflict minerals. It also created a social media influencer campaign to inspire and educate consumers who might not automatically search out information on a corporate site. (See the Q&A with Intel's Teresa Herd.)

The Millennial generation "is looking to us to do the right thing", wrote Carolyn Duran, Intel's supply chain director and conflict minerals programme manager, in a blog post:

> In fact, after being educated about the issue of conflict minerals, more than half of Millennials said they believe technology companies are responsible for taking action on the issue of conflict minerals – more than mineral suppliers, governments, consumers or NGOs. The question isn't will Millennials care about this topic, but when.[37]

Q&A Teresa Herd, vice-president global creative director for Intel

Teresa Herd oversees all creative development for Intel globally.

Q: What makes the work Intel is doing interesting from a sustainability and creative point of view?

A: One of the reasons I joined Intel was because I really wanted to work for a company that was doing something great in the world. Intel, not just from a sustainability standpoint but also from the products that we make, they are enabling the most amazing things. If it turns on and it is connected Intel is somewhere in there – either by powering the device or if it is powering a data centre somewhere – we're part of it. We have a legacy in this area – we were there in the early days helping give Stephen Hawking his voice, for example. I never wake up and think, wow how am I going to spin this idea!

Q: Has sustainability given technology a good story to tell?

A: For a long time it was enough for Intel to talk about the processors inside our PCs – the classic Intel Inside line – but as time went on a new generation of consumers just took that for granted. We realised that if all we talked about was Intel Inside then we were going to die. If people don't care about the brand then they aren't going to care about the processor.

So, when we looked at what we were powering – from the Hubble telescope to the Mars Rover to the Space Shuttle – it became clear that nobody knew these stories. We realised that we had to stop talking about Intel Inside and focus on what Intel was doing outside. That includes issues like Conflict-Free – after all this is a life-and-death experience for some people so making a better life for people who are at the start of mining for the critical things that we all need is a powerful part of explaining what Intel is about.

Conflict-Free and other corporate responsibility work fit perfectly into this narrative and offered an experiential story that taps directly into what younger generations care about today. They don't care so much about the stuff. They care more about what can I do with it and what type of experience can I have interacting with it.

Q: How did Conflict-Free move from a reputation and corporate social responsibility issue to a creative story?

A: Intel's leaders cared a great deal about this issue. So marketing came to us [in creative] saying we want to tell the story and we want Millennials to care.

We know that Millennials do tend to care more about cultural issues once they know about them, but we weren't sure how much they really knew about the issues around Conflict-Free. We'd already made a documentary showing the lives of the miners in the Congo but we felt we needed a different approach to inform Millennials.

So we thought about using influencers. The question for us then was how could we tap into the Millennial reach offered by influencers in a way that would be authentic?

I knew that unboxing videos were a trend online so we built on that idea and went to some unboxing YouTube celebs who had big tech followings. We had them unbox the actual minerals that go into making a processor. We thought: "What if we could get those guys to care and become advocates for Conflict-Free?"

The tech influencers we approached agreed to do the unboxing even though they didn't know what to expect. We told them we were sending them something new and then we delivered them a laptop in a package complete with dirt and the minerals [each tagged with an explanation of their role in making the product]. In that package we also sent a laptop complete with a video that autoplayed when they opened it. The video told the story of Conflict-Free minerals in the Congo where we source our materials and the miners' lives they affected.

They were all completely blown away. None of them had any idea of the issues behind sourcing the product that they use and review every day. The reactions we got were completely authentic – that was very important to us.

At that point things really took off – it was a great use of using influencers that grabbed the interest of tech enthusiasts and that then moved out into the broader population.

Q: Essentially you were able to take what once was seen as a stakeholder conversation and turn it into a social media brand campaign. That's hard because often marketing and comms are afraid of telling those stories. Are there lessons you've learned about making this work with other issues?

A: I always try and understand what the business really wants and needs to accomplish. At first the business just wanted more videos to show the conflict in the Congo, but I believed that wasn't going to resonate with the audience they wanted to engage with. We had to create a new narrative. We had to make a piece of content that would really break through this often sceptical group. Also you have to be realistic about your audience. We couldn't hope to reach all Millennials. That would take a very big budget that we did not have. We had to think of the best way of getting our message into the heads and hearts of those people who will really care about technology and then share story of Conflict-Free on their own.

Q: You've mentioned the importance of authenticity. How does that give a social media campaign more currency?

A: It's best when your cause is legitimate, one that people will really care about it. Ours was. People are hit with so much information, in order to get them to not only pay attention but to take action they have to really care. Once you find the right influencers to deliver the message and you tell them what you have done to make a difference they will share your story because they can see the actual impact it can have. We knew we had success by their desire to share this beyond our campaign. Now they spread the message on their own.

Notes

1 www.nielsen.com/us/en/press-room/2014/global-consumers-are-willing-to-put-their-money-where-their-heart-is.html
2 http://fashionrevolution.org/about/2016-impact/
3 www.forbes.com/sites/mikeotoole/2016/01/05/at-everlane-transparent-is-the-new-black/#2da36fd773ef

4 http://news.averydennison.com/press-release/corporate/avery-dennison-and-evrythng-switch-apparel-industry-10-billion-products-worl
5 www.nytimes.com/2016/07/18/business/media/organic-valley-traces-milk-back-from-table-to-farm.html
6 https://www.nytimes.com/2016/07/18/business/media/organic-valley-traces-milk-back-from-table-to-farm.html
7 www.dailymail.co.uk/news/article-2092127/Jamie-Oliver-Victory-McDonalds-stops-using-pink-slime-burger-recipe.html
8 https://www.campaignlive.co.uk/article/mcdonalds-honest-approach-fast-food/1343221
9 http://burgerbusiness.com/
10 www.campaignlive.co.uk/article/news-analysis-mcdonalds-asking-trouble/652861
11 http://time.com/3501921/mcdonalds-transparency-campaign/
12 https://www.fastcompany.com/3064068/chipotle-eats-itself
13 www.nytimes.com/2012/02/10/business/media/chipotle-ad-promotes-sustainable-farming.html
14 https://www.newyorker.com/business/currency/what-does-the-scarecrow-tell-us-about-chipotle
15 Ibid.
16 www.forbes.com/sites/henrymiller/2015/12/14/chipotle-the-long-defeat-of-doing-nothing-well/
17 https://www.fastcompany.com/3064068/chipotle-eats-itself
18 www.adweek.com/brand-marketing/ad-day-chipotles-latest-epic-animated-film-actually-cry-help-172392/
19 https://harpers.org/archive/1992/08/the-new-free-trade-heel/
20 www.nytimes.com/1996/06/27/business/a-sweetheart-becomes-suspect-looking-behind-those-kathie-lee-labels.html
21 http://money.cnn.com/1998/05/12/companies/nike/
22 www.nytimes.com/1998/05/13/business/international-business-nike-pledges-to-end-child-labor-and-apply-us-rules-abroad.html
23 www.bloomberg.com/news/articles/2004-09-19/online-extra-nikes-new-game-plan-for-sweatshops
24 https://www.theguardian.com/business/2005/apr/14/ethicalbusiness.money
25 www.theguardian.com/environment/green-living-blog/2012/jul/06/activism-nike
26 www.sustainablebrands.com/news_and_views/articles/nike-gap-target-among-founders-sustainable-apparel-coalition
27 www.nikeresponsibility.com/report/content/chapter/manufacturing
28 www.theguardian.com/sustainable-business/nike-supply-chain-measures-up
29 www.slate.com/articles/business/the_grind/2016/08/nike_s_supply_chain_doesn_t_live_up_to_the_ideals_of_its_girl_effect_campaign.html
30 http://thegreensupplychain.com/news/16-05-24-3.php?cid=10743
31 www.manufacturing.net/news/2016/05/nike-plans-fewer-better-factories-meet-environmental-goals
32 https://www.techrepublic.com/article/how-conflict-minerals-funded-a-war-that-killed-millions/
33 https://www.intel.co.uk/content/www/uk/en/corporate-responsibility/conflict-minerals-white-paper.html
34 www.theguardian.com/sustainable-business/intel-conflict-minerals-ces-congo-electronics
35 www.huffingtonpost.com/entry/intel-conflict-free-minerals_us_569520e5e4b05b3245da6ea7
36 https://consciouscompanymedia.com/the-new-economy/how-intel-cut-conflict-minerals-from-its-supply-chain/
37 www.triplepundit.com/2016/01/conflict-free-effect-better-society-better-business/

Chapter 6

Leaders needed

Every movement needs leaders, and sustainable business is no exception – not least because of the role that companies will have to play in order to develop and deliver a sustainable future.

What motivates corporate sustainable leadership varies from company to company. Some see sustainability as an obvious way to cut costs. Others realise that sustainability can open new markets and deliver new business. A growing number of business leaders understand that a commitment to the environment and society over and above the pursuit of profit is baked into their purpose – aka what they stand for. Whatever their motivation, leaders who are committed to sustainability play an important role in helping companies win public trust.

The influential GlobeScan/SustainAbility Sustainability Leaders Report – an annual survey of more than 900 global sustainability executives and consultants – underlines the importance of executive leadership and vision. The top companies listed in the 2017 Survey – Unilever, Patagonia, Interface, IKEA, Marks & Spencer, Natura and Tesla – are all led or founded by people with a singular sustainability drive.

Globescan and SustainAbility noted:

> Aligning sustainability strategy with internal culture and values and integrating purpose via a common brand promise are perceived as two key drivers of corporate leadership. . . . In the case of Unilever, vocal support of sustainability by senior leadership is the single most important factor accounting for its outsized reputation.[1]

Few would argue with Unilever's top-ranked position in the 2017 GlobeScan/SustainAbility survey. And few would disagree that the biggest catalyst for its sustainability commitment has been the leadership of CEO Paul Polman.

A great deal of ink has been spilled documenting Paul Polman's time at the helm of Unilever. This book won't rehash all that has been written about his leadership, but it is worth considering just how sustainability action has helped Unilever's brands build trust with consumers and drive sales in the process.

Polman became chief executive of Unilever in 2009, having worked at Nestlé and P&G. His commitment to sustainability had been forged during those years and he knew it involved more than just environmental practices – we must also tackle "poverty, disease, nutrition, the quality of women's lives", he wrote in a P&G sustainability report from 2000.[2]

Polman wasted no time informing investors that Unilever would put as much stock in the future of the planet as it did its own revenues and profits. One of his first acts was refusing to publish quarterly profit updates.[3] In place of short-term updates, the company undertook a process of long-term sustainable thinking that was first unveiled in 2010 as the Unilever Sustainable Living Plan.

Its central focus was simple but ambitious: to double turnover by 2020 while improving the health and well-being of a billion people, halving the company's environmental impact, and enhancing the livelihoods of people across the value chain.

As *Guardian Sustainable Business* described it:

> Unilever's plan has three distinctive features: It covers social and economic, as well as environmental challenges, all Unilever's products and brands are included, not just a few. It also covers the company's entire value chain, from sourcing raw materials to consumer use of its products and their disposal. With thousands of products that are used 2bn times a day in more than 280 countries, this represents a massive undertaking.[4]

From the very start Unilever was clear that it couldn't meet the goals set out in the Sustainable Living Plan just through its own activities. A great deal rested on changing the way consumers behaved. That's where marketing mattered. In 2010 Unilever expanded the role of chief marketing officer Keith Weed to include all sustainability communication as well as internal and external communications.

As Weed told *Fast Company* in a 2015 interview:

> You can't have marketing in one corner "selling more stuff" and sustainability in another trying to save the world. Bring them together because they are two sides of the same coin. Let's try and do marketing in such a way that we are addressing real social challenges.[5]

The first step was to develop an understanding internally about sustainability and what Unilever stood for. To achieve this Unilever engaged with NGOs, academics, governments and so-called key opinion formers. As described in Chapter 4, the company created an internal crowdsourced platform to get feedback from external experts about sustainability goals. It continues to provide sustainability leadership training including encompassing issues such as reducing food waste, empowering women and reducing deaths from mosquito-borne diseases. By 2017 the sustainability leadership programme had been completed by its senior leaders was being rolled out to include 400 vice presidents across the global business.[6]

At the same time Unilever was both developing the sustainability credentials of its corporate brand and its consumer brands. As Weed described in the same *Fast Company* interview:

> The real thing that has happened in the last five years is transparency with the internet. . . . People are either genuinely interested in what the brand behind the brand is or want to find out if there are any issues with the brand behind the brand. If you have a vacuum, anything can fill it. So the thought was, we need to communicate what we believe Unilever stands for and is trying to achieve with consumers.[7]

In 2013, Unilever launched a corporate brand online platform called Project Sunlight. Its goal was to highlight the sustainability work Unilever's brands were doing and to promote sustainable living to consumers.

Project Sunlight was launched with a short film: *Why Bring a Child into this World?* that sought to portray sustainable living in an aspirational light. Unilever also teamed up with the *Guardian* to produce a native advertising campaign – Live Better Challenge – to take Project Sunlight out to a larger consumer audience. Project Sunlight (which later was rebranded as Bright Future) became a content driver for Unilever's Facebook and Twitter platforms and was shared selectively on the social media pages of some of its consumer brands.

Unilever was also one of the founding corporate supporters of Collectively, a non-profit digital platform targeted at Millennials that grew out of conversations about sustainable living at the 2013 World Economic Forum gathering in Davos.

Yet despite the sustainability commitment at a corporate level, it took some time for sustainability to become a driver of communication at a brand level despite the legacy of Dove and the sustainability credentials gained through the 2001 acquisition of Ben & Jerry's Ice Cream.

Part of the problem seemed to be getting Unilever's marketers to buy into sustainability as a point of differentiation in the marketplace. By 2014, Unilever's sustainable living brands (those designated by the company as being furthest along the journey towards reducing their environmental footprint and increasing their positive social impact) were starting to demonstrate their potential – they accounted for half of the company's growth and were growing twice as fast as other brands in its portfolio. Yet, when Karen Hamilton, Unilever's global vice president for sustainable business, spoke at a marketing conference in London in 2015, she explained that Unilever was having problems convincing marketers of its sustainability strategy.

"We do regular staff surveys to check our progress around sustainability and marketing is 20 percentage points behind the rest of our business when it comes to embracing these changes," she told the conference, adding: "Marketers know we are asking them to think in a completely different mindset and that can be quite daunting."[8]

Hamilton's frank assessment of how the marketing community viewed sustainability was hardly surprising to anyone following sustainability communication in business, but it would have caused a few raised eyebrows at a company that was staking its corporate reputation on being the most sustainable in the business.

The reality for Unilever, and every other company for that matter, is that delivering on sustainability commitments when they've spent decades cultivating a culture of "Don't worry, just keep spending" is no easy task.

Unilever's Sustainable Living Plan has struggled to meet some of its ambitious standards; for example, it has had to push back its goal of halving its products' environmental impact to 2030 from the original 2020 timetable.[9] Many of the goals are on track, though, and gradually more and more of Unilever's brands have found their own sustainability niche to make them resonate with consumers.

As noted in other chapters, Dove has continued its celebration of female self-esteem with its long-running Real Beauty campaigns and these have reached wider global audiences through YouTube, Facebook and Instagram. Persil has embraced the social issue of kid's outdoor playtime with Dirt Is Good and created a short film that has been shared extensively through social media. Knorr has helped tackle iron deficiency for mothers in Nigeria. Hellman's has created a new type of plastic bottle to reduce wastage and described the process through Facebook illustrations. Even Axe/Lynx – the deodorant brand renowned for appealing to teenage boys through sexualised advertising – has tackled important societal issues like young male suicide in new social media campaigns.[10]

Embracing sustainability themes throughout a brand portfolio as broad as Unilever's would have been impossible without executive leadership and a commitment to put sustainability at the heart of business performance. But even Paul Polman probably wouldn't have guessed that sustainability could be a factor in saving Unilever from a hostile corporate takeover.

Yet it was just that – specifically the importance of preserving Unilever's long-term value focus and the commitment to developing sustainable brands – that was one of the factors underpinning the executive board's fierce rebuff of a $143 billion takeover bid by Kraft Heinz in February 2017.[11] It should be noted, however, that the Kraft bid renewed pressure on the Unilever board to deliver short-term rewards to shareholders that has resulted in a broad strategic rethink of the company structure and its food and spreads business.[12]

Kraft, for its part, realised it needed to place more value on sustainability and purpose. Soon after the failed bid it announced a $200 million investment in corporate social responsibility.[13]

A singular sustainability focus

While leaders at companies such as Unilever, Patagonia and Natura have embedded sustainability throughout their operations, other chief executives have chosen to focus on a specific sustainability issue. In the case of AT&T, its commitment to stopping Americans from texting while driving became not just a corporate cause but also a national movement.

In 2010, as AT&T CEO Randall Stephenson has described to the media, a person he knew very well caused an accident while texting and driving.[14] The episode affected him personally and also made him realise the responsibility that his company had to address what is an increasingly deadly issue in our connected society. The smartphone "is a product we sell and it's being used inappropriately" he explained at a 2012 conference.

Randall's response was to mobilise the not-inconsiderable might of AT&T's marketing and communication resources towards two goals: reducing the number of automobile crashes caused by texting while driving, and promoting advocacy to demonstrate that texting is just as dangerous as drinking and driving.

The result was It Can Wait, an awareness-building initiative launched in 2010 that, over the next six years, would expand in reach and grow in ambition to the extent that AT&T's mobile carrier competitors also embraced the campaign. Stephenson told CBS in 2013:

> Every CEO in the industry that you talk to recognizes that this is an issue that needs to be dealt with. I think we all understand that pooling our resources with one consistent message is a lot more powerful than all four of us having different messages and going different directions.[15]

Inside AT&T, It Can Wait has been woven into the corporate fabric. All employees who receive a company-issued phone must sign a code of conduct that now includes a pledge never to text behind the wheel.[16] Externally, AT&T educated consumers about the dangers of texting and driving, and encouraged them to embrace its pledge, through social media campaigns (organised around the hashtag #ItCanWait), community outreach and a poignant documentary film directed by Werner Herzog.

By 2013, AT&T "de-branded" itself from It Can Wait because it had become a social movement. At that point it had won support from 1,500-plus organisations while more than 8 million people had pledged via the It Can Wait website not to text and drive.

CVS refuses to go up in smoke

US retailer, CVS Health, chose to take its own single-issue stand in 2014 by banning tobacco sales from its stores. The decision involved far more risk than AT&T's It Can Wait because CVS knew it would cost the company $2 billion in annual sales.

Nevertheless, after months of discussions, the company's executive team, led by CEO Larry Merlo and supported by Pharmacy President Helen Foulkes, came to realise that "continuing to sell cigarettes had become untenable for a company that was simultaneously trying to sell itself as a health care giant," as *Fortune* described the decision.[17]

It was also a bold decision because, unlike the industry support afforded to AT&T's moral stand, no other major pharmacy followed CVS's lead. Speaking at a marketing conference in 2016, Norman de Greve, head of marketing at CVS, explained that despite having to going it alone, the decision made sense because it proved the company would back up its written purpose with real action. "Selling cigarettes and antibiotics in the same store is just wrong," said de Greve, whose father died of lung cancer when he was only seven years old.

CVS's cause was lauded by then First Lady Michelle Obama, former New York mayor Michael Bloomberg and Microsoft co-founder and public health advocate Bill Gates among others.[18] It was further promoted by a comprehensive social media campaign – #OneGoodReason – that encouraged people to tweet or post on Facebook and Instagram why they wanted to stop smoking. More than 500,000 consumers visited a dedicated page offering advice on quitting smoking and 260,000 people sought help from counsellors at CVS.

A year after stubbing out its cigarette sales, revenue from pharmacy benefits management services (third-party handling of prescriptions) had jumped 11.9 percent, and the company had secured $11 billion in new contracts – in no small part due to brand boost it received from its sustainable stand.

As de Greve explained to *Adweek*,

> I cannot think of another example in corporate America where a company sacrificed $2 billion of revenue for what they felt was the right thing to do. It's a stunning thing. And we know these facts are true, that more purpose-driven companies, a) Millennials and consumers want to do business with . . . and b) it's great for recruiting. It proved out for us in both of those ways.[19]

In 2016, CVS doubled down on its anti-smoking commitment with a five-year $50 million initiative to help deliver the nation's first tobacco-free generation called Be The First. The campaign aimed to cut the national youth smoking rate by 3 percent, reduce the number of new youth smokers by

10 percent and double the number of college campuses that ban tobacco usage. It comprised comprehensive education, advocacy, tobacco control and healthy behaviour programming in partnership with a number of civic organisations committed to combatting what is still the leading preventable cause of disease and death in the United States.[20]

Aetna focuses its mind and embraces sleep

Can yoga and mindfulness in the workplace increase productivity and save money? If you ask Aetna's CEO Mark Bertolini the answer would be a resounding "Om".

Back in 2004, Bertolini, then a senior executive at the health insurance provider, was involved in a near-death skiing accident that left him with five fractured vertebrae in his neck and catastrophic nerve damage to his arm. To handle the pain as he recuperated, Bertolini took the cocktail of painkillers prescribed to him by his doctors but he remained in constant pain. After a year of suffering he ditched the drugs and went in search of alternative therapies.

Bertolini discovered yoga and quickly became a fan of its structured philosophy of strength and stretching as well as its culture and history. Soon he found himself drawn to the meditation and mindfulness benefits that yoga also provides. The effect that yoga and mindfulness mediation had on his ability to manage pain was a revelation to him – so much so that, after becoming CEO in 2012, Bertolini started reshaping the culture of Aetna with what *The New York Times* described as a "series of eyebrow-raising moves".[21]

First, he made free yoga and meditation classes available to Aetna employees. To do so he enlisted the American Viniyoga Institute, which advocates a form of yoga that involves breathing techniques and gentle poses. For the meditation programme, Aetna turned to a Florida consultancy that takes its inspiration from Jon Kabat-Zinn, a molecular biologist who has helped popularise mindfulness.

When management reviewed Aetna's financial performance for 2012, paid medical claims per employee had dropped by 7.3 percent, resulting in $9 million in savings. Since then, they have fluctuated year to year but still remain about 3 percent lower than they were before yoga and meditation were introduced at the company.

By 2015, more than one-quarter of the company's workforce of 50,000 had participated in at least one class, and, on average, they reported a 28 percent reduction in their stress levels, a 20 percent improvement in sleep quality and a 19 percent reduction in pain. Aetna also contends these employees are more productive to the tune of $3,000 per employee per year.[22]

Other wellness initiatives contributed to these health savings, but Bertolini was so convinced of the importance that yoga and meditation played in Aetna's mind and body fabric that he began offering the same classes to the businesses that contract with Aetna for their health insurance.

Bertolini probably didn't realise it at the time, but he was making Aetna a leader in wellness, what *The New York Times* called "a movement that is quietly spreading through the business world." It noted that companies like Google offer emotional intelligence courses for employees. General Mills has a meditation room in every building on its corporate campus. And even buttoned-up Wall Street firms like Goldman Sachs and BlackRock are teaching meditation on the job.[23]

Having embraced meditation, Aetna turned its attention to the issue of sleep in order to shape a happier and more productive workplace. In what the US Centers for Disease Control and Prevention calls a "public health problem" more than one third of Americans get less than the recommended six hours of nightly sleep.[24]

Not surprisingly, a lack of sleep at home has a knock-on effect in the workplace. One 2016 McKinsey survey of 196 business leaders found that 43 percent said say they don't get enough sleep at least four nights a week with nearly six out of 10 saying they don't sleep enough at least three nights a week.[25]

For Aetna, sleep represented the third pillar (along with diet and exercise) of a healthy workforce. Just as the company had identified both yoga and mindfulness as sustainability priorities so it created a programme to help employees get more sleep – offering them up to $500 a year if they got at least seven hours of sleep per night. As Bertolini explained to CNBC, "If they can prove they get 20 nights of sleep for seven hours or more in a row, we will give them $25 a night, up $500 a year."[26] To help employees keep track of their sleep patterns, the company offered Fitbit fitness trackers along with education resources.

The success of Aetna's internal wellness initiatives provided the insurer with an impressive sustainability story to communicate. Using Tumblr the company hosted a 30-day mindfulness challenge (#Mindful30) in January 2016 and enlisted bloggers to share tips and help add mindfulness to daily routines. It also launched the Healthy Sleep Matters campaign, which featured native advertising on *The New York Times* website and HuffPost, as well as YouTube videos and further Tumblr coverage that included a range of guidance, links and infographics to help people embrace healthy sleep as part of their lifestyle.[27] One of the featured videos, which was viewed more than 1.5 million times in a 12-month period, recounted the breakthrough moment for three people when they finally recalled their dreams after years of sleep deprivation that had prevented them from remembering.[28]

REI's outsider stance

Showing leadership on an issue as thorny as responsible consumption is challenge when the modus operandi of most companies is to sell more products. Patagonia has succeeded in this area through its Don't Buy This Jacket and Worn Wear initiatives (described in more detail in Chapter 8) but perhaps the most successful demonstration of how a company can show leadership in this area comes from REI, the outdoor gear cooperative.

In the summer of 2015, the senior executives at REI were brainstorming how they should approach the upcoming winter holiday season – especially the monster one-day consumer frenzy the day after Thanksgiving known as Black Friday.

In recent years many in the media have turned against the Black Friday concept, not least because, each year, TV footage captures how the rush to get bargains brings out the worst in shoppers. Black Friday also puts a serious strain on employees. So, with these issues in mind, the REI team hit on a pretty radical idea. What if it shut its doors on the busiest shopping day of the year and gave its employees a day off with full pay to go and enjoy the great outdoors?

For many retailers this would have seemed like economic suicide but, as the executives would make the case to CEO Jerry Stritzke, REI's cooperative success depended more on long-term members than a one-day feeding frenzy. What's more, the company's whole purpose had been established around exploring and enjoying nature. As REI's vice president of brand stewardship and impact, Alex Thompson, told the Sustainable Brands conference in 2016, "It's crucial to reflect on the foundation on which you are built."

Stritzke was quickly won over and the #OptOutside campaign was born. It launched in October 2015 with a print ad in *The New York Times* followed by TV and online adverts featuring Stritzke explaining why closing all 143 stores for the day made good sense for employees and the community.

It was the social media effect, though, that really kicked #OptOutside into overdrive. Using the hashtag #OptOutside, REI and its agencies created a meme generator that encouraged Twitter, Facebook and Instagram users to share images and videos related to their own outdoor experiences. #OptOutside took a life of its own independent of REI as people started sharing their love for the outdoors in general.

Ultimately #OptOutside became a movement that 1.4 million people and 170 other companies and organisations would embrace.[29] The National Park Service opened its doors for free entry all over the country on that day and, to inspire outdoor action, the campaign site offered advice on local options for exploring trails and parks.

By the time Black Friday had rolled around again in 2016, #OptOutside had taken on ever greater stature. Other brands joined the effort, including Subaru of America, which provided a fleet of vehicles in New York so dog owners could take their pets out walking in nature for the day. Google worked with REI to support outdoor-focused non-profits while competitors like Burton, KEEN, and Yeti supported #OptOutside with social media outreach. *Ad Age* wrote:

> REI's move signals a massive shift in the way companies are doing business and marketing themselves. The new reality is that as customers become

more skilled at, and have better technology for, managing their many brand relationships, they will weed out or ignore companies that fail to sufficiently understand their needs and deliver value against them. This is the new consumerism – empowered, entrepreneurial and enabled.[30]

Despite its enormous online success, as Thompson told me,

This was not designed as a social media or comms campaign. It was a business decision to dig deep into the values of the organisation and show what we stand for. There were no sales goals. Our one measure of success was how well it resonated with employees.

Ad Age agreed: "REI's much-lauded decision is an example of what happens when a brand has a truly empathetic understanding of its customers and uses that understanding to create experiences that customers value."[31]

Q&A with Alex Thompson, Vice President, brand stewardship and impact REI

Q: Where did the idea for Opt Outside come from?

A: It came from within REI. The idea to shut down was likely shared by many retail staff within the organisation over many years but it surfaced formally and gained life as #OptOutside during the second year of CEO Jerry Stritzke's tenure. He laid down a challenge for us to think differently about the holiday period – to signal simply and loudly what we stand for. A group came forward with what some would describe as a heretical idea for a retailer but we are fortunate that our CEO showed trust and saw the potential. Very often, our job as brand builders is to identify and unearth ideas that might already exist. The magic is in asking whether they tie deeply to the culture of an organisation. When that culture matches external sentiment or cultural pressures, that's when special things can happen, as we found with #OptOutside.

Q: Was it hard to get buy in initially?

A: Having a CEO who wanted us to find the edges of what was comfortable was critical but, by his own admission, when we signed off the concept Jerry definitely felt there might be a chance that this would be met with derision in business community. Secondly, the governance structure of the co-op is pertinent. We had to explain the idea to the board of directors – the elected members of the co-op, which includes 16 million people. The board of directors had the responsibility of deliberating and signing off the concept. It was a tense meeting when that happened, given the expected revenue loss, but I will never forget it.

Q: Why was it important to inspire employees first?

A: As with any complicated effort, having an incredibly clear values framework behind whatever you're trying to do is vital. You have to boil an idea down to its essence to find whether it has authenticity, strength and that it can weather the challenges it will face.

We very consciously set no brand or comms metrics whatsoever for #OptOutside and we didn't have any business metrics. We decided that if employees – the 12,000 people who work for the co-op – experienced this as helping them live their lives in a more full and rounded way at a time of the year that had lost its cultural meaning, then that would be deemed a success.

The first time we shared this information was with 300 of our store managers a month before the announcement. It received a standing ovation and there were tears. Amazingly, those leaders held onto that announcement without telling anyone in a very small industry. Then, when we finally announced the initiative our CEO did so first in a letter to all our employees.

Q: Was that because your employees are REI's best ambassadors?

A: In a word, yes. They are the biggest users of the gear we sell, for one thing, but we also went to our employees first because it was the right thing to do – both culturally and because it was designed for them. We wouldn't tell anyone else what we were doing for our employees before we told them.

To make a big initiative a success you very much have to engage your employee group and you have to build a deep understanding with them of what you want to achieve. We operate in such a fast-moving environment nowadays that, unless employees understand your values, your motivation and where you are coming from, an initiative like #OptOutside would likely fall at the first hurdle.

Q: Why do you think that consumers and society validated REI's stand on this issue?

A: It was authentic to who we are and have always been. #OptOutside was, at its core, about presenting a simple choice – to enjoy life outside. In its expression, the initiative tapped into fairly deep sense of unease about the choices people are making. We all feel the risk that we are sleep-walking into ways of behaving that take us away from the things we enjoy the most. And we are seeing that unease in the political discourse and overarching tonality in media. That partly why there is a fundamental shift in the way that people view the responsibility of various institutions – including government and business. Nowadays, organisations are expected to step into spaces where they haven't had the opportunity or liberty to speak before. That is becoming a very significant factor for any leader to consider.

Q: What role did social media play in shaping #OptOutside?

A: There is no question it played a big role because millions of people joined the movement, but #OptOutside was much more than a social media campaign. At its core it was a business decision – an important choice that REI made to show to its employees what it cares about. No doubt, social media was a really important operating environment. You have to do well there. If you don't, your motivation gets completely lost.

Social media gave us, with a very limited advertising budget (keep in mind we hand back 70 percent of our profits annually) an already connected and wired network of incredibly passionate people. When the idea hit the consciousness of that network it spread like wildfire. And it's worth mentioning that the social media effect was only built after more traditional methods of communication – the letters to our employees, our members and a network of NGOs. But social media helped light the touch paper of popular sentiment. That's when it caught fire. It happened because we had credibility with the people who really counted.

Q: How important was it to give consumers and employees useful information?

A: It was crucial that we made it easy for people to take part. If you consider that we have millions of members and they now have the ability to connect through their smartphones we absolutely saw the opportunity to use these tools to mobilise people. You could retweet and support #OptOutside. You could also signal your intent through social media platforms that you were supporting it. We also had a tool that allowed you to put in your zip code and be offered options to get outside. Importantly many of those trails and parks had been supported and funded by REI in the past.

Q: And REI was backing up words with actions, no?

A: Absolutely. We backed it up with losing millions of dollars of sales. That was a choice we made and so we made it really clear that #OptOutside was about choice for our members. People were feeling more and more uncomfortable with their lack of time and the barriers that existed to making simple choices so we made it easier for them. Social media shortened the distance between thinking you might like to get out and enjoy the outside, being given an opportunity by REI and then actually doing it. Six million people took part in year two.

Q: What has the experience told you about mobilizing a sustainability movement?

A: It's important to understand that most people aren't looking to have a sustainability conversation as packaged by the sustainability intelligentsia and elite. What is really important is to focus on simple human truths and motivations and work out how your sustainability philosophy fits into people's emotions and needs.

Notes

1 www.globescan.com/news-and-analysis/press-releases/press-releases-2017/414-values-innovation-and-transparency-key-to-future-corporate-sustainability-leadership-new-survey-of-experts.html

2 https://newint.org/features/web-exclusive/2017/04/13/inside-unilever-sustainability-myth/

3 www.ft.com/content/e6696b4a-8505-11e6-8897-2359a58ac7a5

4 https://www.theguardian.com/sustainable-business/unilever-sustainable-living-plan

5 https://www.fastcompany.com/3051498/why-unilever-is-betting-big-on-sustainability

6 www.unilever.com/sustainable-living/our-strategy/embedding-sustainability/helping-our-people-drive-sustainable-growth/

7 https://www.fastcompany.com/3051498/why-unilever-is-betting-big-on-sustainability

8 www.thedrum.com/news/2015/07/15/why-unilever-s-marketers-aren-t-embracing-sustainability-and-how-nationwide-became

9 www.ft.com/content/e6696b4a-8505-11e6-8897-2359a58ac7a5

10 https://sustainly.com/content/article/991/lynx-raises-alarm-about-male-suicide-bigger-issues

11 www.ft.com/content/d846766e-f81b-11e6-bd4e-68d53499ed71

12 www.ft.com/content/2a859088-fe78-3796-98a4-a696faa67fb5

13 www.bloomberg.com/news/articles/2017-03-21/kraft-heinz-expands-sustainability-push-after-unilever-rejection

14 www.nytimes.com/2012/09/20/technology/att-chief-speaks-out-on-texting-while-driving.html

15 www.cbsnews.com/news/big-4-cell-phone-carriers-to-team-in-ads-against-texting-while-driving/

16 www.dallasnews.com/business/business/2013/09/21/att-spending-millions-to-get-it-can-wait-message-across

17 http://fortune.com/2015/09/11/cvs-health-helena-foulkes/

18 www.prweek.com/article/1310741/cvs-onegoodreason-social-effort-draws-high-level-support-twitter#8E8sr5Dx6GrHGYWe.99

19 http://www.adweek.com/brand-marketing/cvs-marketing-chief-says-phasing-out-tobacco-helped-prove-companys-purpose-174183/

20 www.usatoday.com/story/money/2016/03/10/cvs-smoking-prevention-campaign/81574276/

21 www.nytimes.com/2015/03/01/business/at-aetna-a-ceos-management-by-mantra.html

22 https://hbr.org/2015/12/the-busier-you-are-the-more-you-need-mindfulness

23 https://www.nytimes.com/2015/03/01/business/at-aetna-a-ceos-management-by-mantra.html

24 www.cdc.gov/features/dssleep/

25 www.mckinsey.com/business-functions/organization/our-insights/the-organizational-cost-of-insufficient-sleep

26 www.cnbc.com/2016/04/05/why-aetnas-ceo-pays-workers-up-to-500-to-sleep.html

27 http://aetna.tumblr.com/

28 www.youtube.com/watch?v=SGpSkKgYFBc&list=PL0ovlWLRVVGsLdkMZu6D0xjFtqfSaAR4Z

29 http://blog.rei.com/news/optoutside-will-you-go-out-with-us/

30 http://adage.com/article/digitalnext/rei-s-optoutside-a-model-future-marketing/301177/

31 http://adage.com/print/301177

Chapter 7

Empower and educate

A "toxic mirror". That's how *Time* magazine described the effect social media can have on teen self-esteem and body confidence.[1] In a 2016 article, it cited academic research that found "robust cross-cultural evidence linking social media use to body image concerns, dieting, body surveillance, a drive for thinness and self-objectification in adolescents."[2]

Women have long been influenced by unrealistic ideals of body image of course. The "cult of thin" perpetuated by the fashion and beauty industry and slavishly promoted by lifestyle media has been an undermining influence for many decades but, as with many other aspects of life, the arrival of social media has exacerbated those trends and influences.

Confronted with this growing crisis, a number of brands have come to realise that self-esteem is an important social sustainability issue – one that, along with the work they are doing promoting racial, gender and sexual equality, they can show leadership in empowering their consumers even as they come to terms with their own responsibility for perpetuating the crisis.

Ironically the first major brand self-esteem project of the social media era was first conceived before social media had really taken hold, and before social concerns had been embraced as a core part of corporate sustainability.

In 2004, Dove, a Unilever brand, was struggling to remain relevant amid increased competition in the soap market. To gain insight into its target market the brand commissioned a study of more than 3,000 women in 10 countries to discover their interests. The study was titled *The Real Truth About Beauty*, and one of the key findings was quite shocking: only 2 percent of the women interviewed considered themselves beautiful.

As Sylvia Lagnado, Dove's brand director, observed at the time:

> The results [of the study] demonstrate the need to present a wider definition of beauty than is currently available to women – regardless of where they live. By doing this, Dove can not only help women feel beautiful every day, we can help them lead more satisfied lives.[3]

So was Dove's Campaign for Real Beauty born, first as a photography exhibition, then expanded into a billboard campaign across Canada, the United

States and the United Kingdom.[4] The billboards showed images of women with two tick-box options next to them, such as "fat or fit?" and "grey or gorgeous?" Viewers were encouraged to send a text with their vote and the rolling tally was displayed on the billboard.

If the billboard campaign seemed a little shallow, it did succeed in driving 1.5 million visitors to the Campaign for Real Beauty website. There they would learn about Dove's partnership with outside organisations like Girls Inc. and the Boys & Girls Clubs of America to boost self-esteem through discussions about online bullying and other teen topics.

"[We were thinking], we have to walk the talk," Sharon MacLeod, vice president of Unilever North America Personal Care, told HuffPost. "We can't just be getting people stirred up; awareness and conversation isn't enough. We actually have to do something to change what's happening."[5]

In 2006, one year after YouTube launched, a new Real Beauty campaign video, *Evolution*, proved a viral sensation, recording 2 million views in just two weeks.[6] It, and a follow-up video titled *Onslaught*, was so successful that Greenpeace parodied the campaign in its hard-hitting attack on Unilever's palm oil sourcing (as recounted in Chapter 2).

Dove had tapped into a real social concern about body image, but it wasn't until 2013, three years after Unilever had unveiled its Sustainable Living Plan, that Dove's self-esteem message really connected with consumers, in the form of a video called *Real Beauty Sketches*, which shot to viral fame in April 2013 and quickly becoming the most-watched video ad of all time.

In its continued attempt to debunk the misconceptions women have about their own physical appearances, Dove arranged for seven women, one at a time, to describe themselves to an FBI-trained forensic sketch artist named Gil Zamora. He couldn't see the women, and the participants did not initially see the drawings he made. For the second part of the experiment, the women's looks were described to the same artist by a random stranger.

At the end the two sets of drawings – one visualised by the women themselves, and the other by the strangers – were placed side-by-side for comparison. Strikingly, the self-visualised sketches were less attractive and focused more on imperfections. The drawings, as described by the stranger, showed younger, prettier faces. The YouTube video ended by capturing the women's reactions as each sketch was presented.

The award-winning campaign caused a huge stir online, with many praising the brand for its touching and original examination of female self-perception. Some critics, however, claimed it was patronising and complained that using a male sketch artist undermined the video's message. Nevertheless, both the positive and negative feedback drove interest in Dove's campaign and traffic to its Self-Esteem Project website.[7]

Later iterations of the Real Beauty campaign took a more overt social media focus. The hashtag-driven #NoLikesNeeded campaign aimed at persuading girls that they shouldn't judge their beauty because of the number of "likes" their selfies get on social media. Dove also launched a self-esteem Pinterest page and ran an inspired Snapchat teen chat campaign.

By any brand campaign measure, Real Beauty was a big success. As of 2017, some 19.4 million young people have interacted with the Dove Self-Esteem Project. More than 625,000 teachers have delivered a Dove self-esteem workshop and more than 1.5 million parents have engaged with the online content. Meanwhile the sale of Dove products has jumped from $2.5 billion to $4 billion since Real Beauty launched. Brand Finance, a business valuation consultancy, estimated in 2016 that Dove was the 10th most valuable beauty brand in the world.[8]

Dove's commercial success thanks to its social sustainability stand was not lost on other brands. In 2014 Under Armour created its own self-esteem campaign, What I Want, featuring supermodel Gisele Bündchen, who, in the campaign video, worked out with a punch bag as online comments about her (not all complimentary) were projected on the walls of the gym.

Even Unilever little brother Axe (known as Lynx in the United Kingdom) embraced self-esteem as it attempted to move beyond its rather juvenile brand history. In the past, one of the biggest criticisms of Dove's Self-Esteem Project was that it couldn't really be authentic when other Unilever brands like Axe/Lynx were sending exactly the opposite message through marketing that objectified women in order to appeal to the fantasies of spotty teenage boys. One of its most famous/infamous adverts, after all, depicted beautiful, scantily clad angels falling out of the sky as they were dragged down to earth through sexual gravitational attraction to a young man wearing Axe/Lynx . . . of course.

However, in 2016 the brand changed its identity with the launch of Men in Progress, a serious UK campaign that portrayed a more compassionate and sensitive vision of masculinity than the chick magnets of the past.

The campaign was based around a series of six black-and-white videos, featuring men addressing the camera. *Like Father Like Son* depicted new fathers talking about their babies, and dads and adult sons discussing their relationship. *Pride* featured a gay rugby professional, a bisexual man and a transgender man. *Nicknames* asked men to reveal what they and others have been called in the past.

Men in Progress was a notable change of direction for Axe/Lynx and part of a repositioning towards Unilever's goal to deliver brands with purpose. Yet it paled in comparison with perhaps the biggest self-esteem campaign in recent years: Like a Girl from the P&G feminine products brand Always.

As with the inception of Dove's Real Beauty, Like a Girl began with the need for a brand refresh (too many girls associated Always with their mothers) and inspiration from a piece of research that revealed most girls in the United States – 72 percent of them according to the study – feel that society limits them, especially during puberty, when their confidence is already low. What's more, women never regain their pre-puberty level of self-esteem. Specifically, the brand discovered that when girls begin to have periods, the event marks the lowest point of confidence in their lives.[9]

Working with the Leo Burnett Agency, Always hit on a new approach to promote self-esteem for young women. The creative idea was a set of videos that turned the description "like a girl" from an insult to a compliment. Directed by documentary filmmaker Lauren Greenfield, the different videos featured different girls taking part in various activities, but the iconic character was a female pitcher who threw incredibly hard and accurately . . . like a girl. The videos proved popular to view and share – the initial one recorded 95 million YouTube views by the end of 2015.

Like Dove, Always sought to back up its female self-esteem bon mots with real action as the brand's head of marketing, Michele Baeten, describes in the Q&A at the end of this chapter. Frankly, if they hadn't offered education, support and mentorship, neither brand would have been able to claim any credibility or authenticity as they sought to win back the trust (and brand loyalty) of the public.

Tech's female trouble

In the summer of 2015, a young computer platform engineer called Isis Wenger agreed to take part in a recruitment poster campaign for her company, OneLogin, that would be featured on San Francisco's public transport system. Little did she know that, within days, she would lead a global social media backlash against sexism and misogyny within Silicon Valley and the technology industry in general.

When the advertising campaign went live Wenger was shocked by a raft of social media comments that questioned whether she could be a real engineer because she is young and attractive. As one man commented on a thread next to a photo of the poster:

> I think they want to appeal to women, but are probably just appealing to dudes. Perhaps that's the intention all along. But I'm curious people with brains find this quote remotely plausible if women in particular buy this image of what a female software engineer looks like.[10]

Some people might have been cowed by the comments. Certainly Wenger wasn't the type of person who would normally seek the limelight. "As a genuine introvert I have never cared much about gaining public attention and I really wasn't prepared for how much everything blew up," she later told TechCrunch[11]. But, as she wrote in a post on the Medium blogging platform in the days after the experience: "The negative opinions about this ad that strangers feel so compelled to share illustrate solid examples of the sexism that plagues tech."[12]

Then she added this call to action for women in tech:

Do you feel passionately about helping spread awareness about tech gender diversity?

Do you not fit the "cookie-cutter mould" of what people believe engineers should look like?

If you answered yes to any of these questions I invite you to help spread the world and help us redefine what an engineer should look like. #ILookLikeAnEngineer.

The reaction was remarkable as women (and men) began sharing pictures using the hashtag to show that engineers do indeed come in all shapes, sizes and colours.

Over the next couple of days companies and prominent individuals with huge social media followings joined in, including Chelsea Clinton, the Girl Scouts, *The New York Times*, Intel, even the United Kingdom's Royal Navy and the Israel Defence Forces.

On the one hand Wenger's accidental viral campaign simply highlighted how deeply ingrained sexism is within the technology industry – a fact that was further demonstrated in 2017 when a blog post written by a former Uber engineer outlining a pattern of sexual harassment at the company prompted many other women to share similar experiences at other Silicon Valley firms.

But on the other hand it also shone a light on a much bigger sustainability problem for all companies. Namely, in an age when technology dominates every area of business there is a chronic shortage of females with the expertise to forge a career in tech.

Surely then, if there was ever an area of sustainability where companies could share their expertise to empower society and win the trust of the public it was in the education of a new generation of Science, Technology, Engineering and Mathematics (STEM)–savvy young women.

According to the US government, less than 25 percent of STEM jobs are filled by women, even though female employees make up about half of the total workforce.[13] Across the Atlantic the situation is equally bleak. In the United Kingdom the proportion of the STEM workforce made up by women is just 21 percent.

This, as you can probably guess, is not a new tale. Take the world of computer science. Ever since the birth of the World Wide Web back in 1991, the number of women employed in computer science has declined even as the economies of the developed world have become increasingly dependent on technology-led talent. By 2020, there will be 1.4 million jobs available in computing-related fields and United States graduates are on track to fill 29 percent of those jobs – but of those jobs just 3 percent will likely be filled by women.

Advocacy groups had been promoting the importance of increasing female representation in STEM jobs since the 1980s, but it wasn't until 2009 that the lack of women in STEM began to resonate through business world conversations. The creation of Ada Lovelace Day, a celebration of women in technology that was named after the world's first computer programmer, helped raise awareness of the issue and put pressure on companies partly by highlighting the lack of women invited to speak at the technology and social media conferences so popular with the corporate world.

At the same time, in the United States, the Obama administration launched its Educate to Innovate campaign with the aim of "moving American students from the middle to the top of the pack in science and math achievement over the next decade."[14] The Obama administration's directive coincided with a change of mindset within companies as they began to view issues like education less as corporate social responsibility and more as an important sustainability concern for the business. In the case of improving female STEM numbers, the business case was easy to make: all major companies already realised that technology was going to shape their future success. To survive and flourish they were going to need a great deal more STEM talent.

For certain sectors, supporting women in STEM was an easy fit. Technology, Internet and telecommunications companies were the first to develop sustainability programmes but, soon, they had been joined by financial services (no doubt spooked by the growth of, and threat posed by, FinTech start-ups), industrial goods and services and even the oil and gas sector.

Corporate enthusiasm for educating the next generation of female STEM graduates can be seen in the way so many companies have lent support to organisations like Girls Who Code, an NGO that aims to close the gender gap in technology. Founded in 2013 with the goal of teaching computer coding skills to 20 school-age girls in New York, Girls Who Code quickly expanded its workshops to train more than 10,000 girls across 42 states in the United States – the vast majority still studying in middle or high school. Along the way, Girls Who Code has attracted nearly $3 million in direct funding from AT&T, Adobe and The Prudential Foundation, and more than 20 leading technology companies have pledged to offer paid internships and other opportunities to girls who have graduated from the Girls Who Code programme.

Companies look to inspire with an eye to hire

In 2009, Time Warner launched its five-year Connect a Million Minds project with the aim of inspiring more than 1 million young people to undertake after-school classes in STEM.[15]

Its focus was very much directed at early teenagers in middle school – the age at which most kids (especially young girls) lose interest in studying STEM subjects. Connect a Million Minds worked with non-profit organisations focused on music, sports, video games, fashion, movies and TV, and social media to provide hands-on learning for kids and demonstrate the connection between STEM and many different areas of work and culture. In doing so the programme aimed to show kids the real value of mathematics and science.

To raise awareness Time Warner donated more than $200 million in public service announcements. But what made the programme really useful (and hence a long-lasting success) was the "Connectory" – an online database that allowed non-profit organisations to publicise their after-school STEM programs so that parents could research after-school programs near them. Over time the Connectory came to list 5,500 non-profit partners who posted almost 12,000 STEM programs across the country.

Tapping into the power of social networks, Connect a Million Minds also created a pledging campaign – partly to spread word of the programme but also to measure its success through real-world validations rather than relying on social media analytics. The pledging campaign asked parents, educators, and mentors to pledge via short videos and posts hosted on the Connect a Million Minds website to connect a child to a hands-on STEM experience.

Connect a Million Minds benefited greatly from celebrity support. NBA hero Magic Johnson and tennis star Sloane Stephens both contributed videos showing how STEM links to sports while other campaign case studies shone a light on cool technology like flying cars. By May 2014 Connect a Million Minds had received more than one million pledges.

Speaking to *Triple Pundit* in 2014, Time Warner Cable's vice-president of Community Investment, Milinda Martin, explained how Connect a Million Minds met both sustainability and corporate social responsibility objectives:

> We need STEM-educated workers for our industry. We know that the U.S. is not training enough students in these skills to the point where there is a gap between open positions and skilled workers taking them – not just in cable, but in all STEM-dependent industries. We also want to positively impact communities, and we know that STEM jobs are high paying and can lift a family out of poverty. We feel that financially stable communities not only are better for the individuals that live in them, but also for the businesses that provide services to them.[16]

Another media and telecom company that understood the importance and social power of STEM was Verizon. In 2013 it launched Powerful Answers (as mentioned in Chapter 4), a crowdsourced campaign that aimed to educate consumers about the ways Verizon's core wireless business helps in the fields of health care, education, sustainability and public safety.

Powerful Answers featured a series of creative video spots and it also invested a good deal of social media capital in creating a dedicated Tumblr site to connect with a younger audience who would have little incentive to search out Verizon's sustainability work on its corporate site.

Not only did Tumblr provide Powerful Answers with a fresh platform, but it also gave Verizon the freedom to create attention-grabbing content and experiment with short-form video snacks and bold banner images that the Tumblr community would appreciate and share.

In 2014, Verizon added a dedicated female STEM focus to its Powerful Answers initiative in the form of the Inspire Her Mind campaign, whose main video grabbed more than 1.3 million views in the first few weeks of being released.

Inspire Her Mind was a collaboration between Verizon and Makers, a women's media and leadership platform comprised of Emmy-nominated documentaries, award-winning web and mobile-first video content, and live events. The main advert was created by AKQA agency and was narrated by Reshma Saujani, founder of Girls Who Code, who recounted the story of a young girl as she experiences growing up in a loving but misguided family culture that reinforces negative female stereotypes and, unwittingly, discourages her from exploring her curiosity in math and science.

The campaign also featured an online site that featured raw and honest testimonials from real women including astronaut Mae Jamison, CEO Linda Alvarado, Google exec Susan Wojcicki and social entrepreneur Marika Shioiri-Clark, who all had to struggle to carve a career in STEM fields.

Other telecom companies have also embraced STEM issues, notably coding. In Europe, Orange has pioneered Supercoders, an annual event held simultaneously in France, Poland, Romania and Spain to teach 10–13 year olds digital literacy and introduce them to coding. Run in conjunction with the European Union's annual Code Week, the Supercoders project builds on other initiatives including Better Internet for Kids.

But when it comes to coding expertise no sector is better placed to help inspire a new generation of kids than technology.

Google's Made With Code project aimed to help girls involved in coding with this simple rallying cry: "Girls start out with a love of science and technology, but lose it somewhere along the way. Let's help encourage that passion in teen girls."[17] The company partnered with the likes of Cartoon Network, Pixar Animation Studies and MIT Media Lab to provide learning resources around computer coding for girls and it looked to engage kids with dedicated Instagram, Tumblr and Twitter accounts.

Google's rival, Microsoft, also has legitimate concerns about the number and quality of smart, tech-savvy employees it will be able to call on in a world whose future and well-being will be shaped by those who understand technology.

In 2012 it launched the YouthSpark programme, a three-year education project that involves partnering with non-profits, schools, governments and other businesses to make computer science education more accessible to more young people, especially those from underrepresented backgrounds.

Initially YouthSpark had a broader educational focus but over time it has put greater emphasis on computer skills and coding. The centrepiece of

YouthSpark is an online hub providing access to information and material around computer science. This includes using the Minecraft virtual world gaming platform (which Microsoft acquired in 2014) as a playground for the simple Hour of Code tutorials created by the Code.org non-profit organisation. The addition of Minecraft has re-energised YouthSpark, invigorating the programme thanks to its longstanding educational credentials. The platform hosts an officially sanctioned education edition that brings Minecraft into classrooms and allows kids to experiment and build worlds and scenarios that can help with subjects including history, geography and architecture – even biology! In 2015, Microsoft extended YouthSpark with a commitment of $75 million in community investments over the next three years.

While most of the recent sustainability education campaigns have focused on improving STEM opportunities, Pearson's Project Literacy had a much broader corporate mandate – namely to promote literacy (including digital literacy) to tackle global poverty. Illiteracy is a global crisis that affects more than 750 million people – that's one in 10 alive today. It also costs the world $1.19 trillion a year.[18]

As part of the ambitious five-year project, the global educational publisher created an online idea bank for people to suggest the best digital literacy solutions being created in the world. The ideas that were submitted were many and varied – from within the company and outside, and from locations around the world. At the time Pearson said it planned to "invest in new collaboration and action" on the literacy challenges being discussed.[19]

In 2016 Pearson revamped Project Literacy specifically to address the United Nations' Sustainable Development Goals about education and poverty. It commissioned agency FCB Inferno to create an awareness-raising campaign titled #ProjectIlliteracy. The centrepiece was an animated video called *The Alphabet of Illiteracy* that explained how global issues such as Ebola, child soldiers, female genital mutilation and homeless have their roots in illiteracy and the lack of a decent education. That video was viewed more than 13 million times in 2016 and won a Cannes Lions Health and Wellness Grand Prix.

Get them when they're young

It's not just tech and telecom companies that have pinned their soft sustainability flags to the STEM mast. Consumer brands – especially those focused on young girls – have also looked to inspire.

GoldieBlox, Mattel and LEGO are just three prominent kids' brands that have grabbed the headlines in recent years as they released STEM-related products.

GoldieBlox was the first to make a media splash. It achieved success from a standing start thanks to the power of crowdfunding and viral social media. A start-up founded by Stanford University engineer Debbie Sterling, GoldieBlox's first toy – a board game to help inspire girls – received huge support on Kickstarter when it was floated on the crowdfunding platform back in 2012.

That drew a good deal of technology and business media attention, but it was the social media reaction to GoldieBlox' first advert that made the company famous (maybe a little infamous, actually) and also struck a big blow against stereotyping of young girls in the games and toy industry. The advert for the game showed three girls creating and executing an elaborate Rube Goldberg machine in their home and garden. But it was the soundtrack for the video that helped send it viral. GoldieBlox had sampled the Beastie Boys' hit song "Girls" – prompting the band to complain because of its use for a commercial purpose. The argument further stoked media interest, which only increased views of the video even after GoldieBlox had replaced "Girls" with a more generic soundtrack.

Against the backdrop of GoldieBlox's newcomer success it was inevitable that other, larger, toy companies would be challenged about their STEM commitments.

Back in 2010 Mattel released a new book: *Barbie: I Can Be a Computer Engineer,* part of what the *Guardian* called a series of gender-stereotype breaking books. Barbie, the icon of high heels and all things pink, might have seemed a strange role model for STEM achievement but, on the surface, the book appeared to be a good attempt to show young girls that any career was achievable.

Unfortunately, anyone who read the book quickly discovered that Barbie was a pretty useless computer engineer. Computer Engineer Barbie was very keen on designing video games but when it came to the coding part she needed boys' help to make it work. Her tech limitations didn't end there. As the narrative progressed our pink heroine managed to infect both her and her sister's computer with a virus and then needed those same tech-savvy boys to fix that problem too.

The book flew under the social media radar until 2014 when it came to the attention of a group of female computer engineers alerted by a blog post written by Pamela Ribbon. Her post "Barbie Fucks It Up Again" went viral and prompted a vitriolic and very funny reaction, including a website, Feminist Hacker Barbie, that encouraged visitors to write new content for the book to "help make Computer Engineer Barbie better."

The backlash was so swift and resonated so far and wide through blogs, social networks and mainstream news publications that Mattel quickly withdrew the book and pledged that all future Barbie titles "will be written to inspire girls' imaginations and portray an empowered Barbie character".[20]

Fast forward to 2016 and Mattel released a new doll: Game Developer Barbie, complete with a laptop featuring "real game code graphics". Game Developer Barbie was part of a range of new inspiring female role model dolls that included Entrepreneur Barbie, Spy Squad Barbie and even a President Barbie that looked remarkably like Hillary Clinton. As Disney's parenting blog Babble described the doll: "In the notoriously male-centric tech world,

Game Developer Barbie is a major step forward when it comes to showing girls there's no such thing as a 'man's world,' because yes, women can do anything, too."[21]

Q&A with Michele Baeten, associate brand director of Always

Q: Where did Like a Girl come from?

A: Ever since the inception of Always, a good 34 years ago, we've had a clear purpose in mind – empowering and advocating women to live life to their full potential. In order to do so, we knew we needed to be there for them from the very first moment when they start their journey being a woman – which is adolescence together with menarche.

We knew that was a very turbulent moment for girls so what the brand has done since the very start is enable education by going into schools – either educating teachers with material or sending substitute teachers into the classroom especially in countries where there still remains a significant stigma or taboo about teaching about menstruation.

We would educate about the period, the cycle and what products to use. Often there wasn't a very good handover from mom to daughter about what they should do.

With the growth of the Internet about 15 years ago we increased our effort to extend our reach around education. We offered information on our website and provided consultants who could answer questions young women might have about the changes they were going through.

We go to over 70 countries globally and we reach 17 million girls with this education. This is done out of goodwill – there was no return on investment on this. When I joined Always four years ago I wondered why we weren't communicating the work we were doing.

At the same time we were going deeper into consumer insight to try and understand what young women struggle with in their life. We discovered that girls' confidence drops significantly at menarche – 51 percent of girls lose confidence at this pivotal point in their lives. Indeed it's the lowest point of confidence a woman will ever experience.

We set out to ask, can we stop the drop in confidence that girls experience at puberty?

Q: Why does Always as a brand need to play that role? A lot of brands wouldn't embrace purpose on this level if there was no obvious return on investment.

A: If you look at P&G's purpose, values and principle – the framework of our existence – it is to touch and improve lives of consumers every day.

Like a Girl came with a clear mindset of what is right. The "sell" to my business partners was on the basis that Like a Girl would drive the brand's relevancy for young women. At the time we were losing brand relevancy with our younger consumers and we were a brand that had a big strength in terms of being function but didn't connect with consumers on an emotional level. So in order to sell-in why doing good was also the right thing from a business standpoint we had to show that our sense of purpose would improve emotional relevancy for the brand.

The advantage we had after 34 years of social-purpose education and other community programs in Africa was that we had the heritage to be at the forefront of the battle to fight this confidence drop. Other brands have in the past tried to come into social responsibility without taking responsibility and they have fallen flat because they weren't doing the right thing even as they tried to talk about doing the right thing.

Q: Was this the perfect initiative for a time when people are sharing emotional relevancy on social media in ways they never had before?

A: When we launched, we decided to start small in order to prove that purpose could build brand relevance. We started with launching the Like a Girl film on YouTube – as social as you can get – and we posted it on Facebook and had an activation plan based on bringing in some influencers to get it off the ground. There wasn't a lot of investment at the start but it took off like wildfire because of its authenticity, and because we could back up what we were saying with action.

Once we saw that Like a Girl had captured the imagination of the public we started fuelling the campaign and, in just 20 days, we moved from a one-market launch to a 20-market launch. Furthermore, we surveyed across 10,000 girls in our top 10 markets before and after the campaign. What we found was that after the campaign, 76 percent considered "Doing something like a girl" a positive phrase compared to just 19 percent before the campaign began.

That's when we knew it had the potential to change society and our data also showed us it could change male perceptions. We knew we had to scale this on a much greater level and that's when the decision to take Like a Girl to the Superbowl was taken.

Q: This was your first taste of social responsibility in marketing. What are the lessons Like a Girl taught you?

A: That is a tough question. I'd say always be true to who you are as a brand. But you can only do this when you have people with real passions that can make real emotions ring true for the consumer. My team is consumed, obsessed and in love with the consumer space they work in. Their passion to help girls overcome the drop in self-esteem and this is what has driven this campaign through its different stages and help it stay energised.

Q: How do you think purpose marketing will grow in the future?

A: We have tremendous power as advertisers and brand builders. It's a missed opportunity if you don't apply your brand to do good. That said, it has to be done in a way that is authentic for your brand. And you have to be doing the work in order to have the permission to be authentic.

Notes

1 http://time.com/4459153/social-media-body-image/
2 www.researchgate.net/publication/298794212_A_systematic_review_of_the_impact_of_the_use_of_social_networking_sites_on_body_image_and_disordered_eating_outcomes
3 www.clubofamsterdam.com/contentarticles/52 Beauty/dove_white_paper_final.pdf
4 www.adweek.com/news/advertising-branding/doves-new-billboards-criticize-way-media-discusses-female-athletes-looks-172688
5 http://www.huffingtonpost.co.uk/entry/dove-real-beauty-campaign-turns-10_n_4575940
6 www.youtube.com/watch?v=iYhCn0jf46U
7 www.dove.com/uk/dove-self-esteem-project.html
8 www.theguardian.com/fashion/2017/may/15/beauty-giant-dove-body-shaped-bottles-repair-damage
9 www.adweek.com/news/advertising-branding/how-always-brand-director-turned-ad-movement-shattered-stereotypes-167468
10 http://www.adweek.com/digital/ilooklikeanengineer-movement-sparks-outpouring-solidarity-techs-diversity-166249/
11 https://techcrunch.com/2015/08/03/ilooklikeanengineer-aims-to-spread-awareness-about-gender-diversity-in-tech/
12 https://thecoffeelicious.com/you-may-have-seen-my-face-on-bart-8b9561003e0f
13 http://www.esa.doc.gov/reports/women-stem-gender-gap-innovation
14 https://obamawhitehouse.archives.gov/issues/education/k-12/educate-innovate
15 www.connectamillionminds.com/
16 https://www.triplepundit.com/2014/11/connect-million-minds-improving-stem-skills/
17 https://www.madewithcode.com/about/
18 https://www.projectliteracy.com/about
19 https://www.projectliteracy.com/about
20 https://www.theguardian.com/books/2014/nov/21/barbie-computer-engineer-story-withdrawn-sexist-mattel
21 https://www.babble.com/parenting/mattel-knocks-it-out-of-the-park-with-new-game-developer-barbie/

Chapter 8

Inspiring behaviour change

Collaborating with the crowd. Radical transparency. Understanding the needs of community in order to provide new tools and services to empower them. Having strong leadership to make sustainability the centre of business strategy. Companies will need all of these strengths as they demonstrate their value in the coming years to consumers and to society as a whole. Proving that value will be crucial in winning back trust but it will also be crucial in helping companies inspire the consumer behaviour change necessary for our world to survive and flourish in the coming decades.

Most sustainability experts acknowledge that comprehensive system change is needed throughout industry sectors and across society for sustainable business to have a truly positive impact on the world. That involves greater collaboration with competitors and relevant external organisations, including even the most critical NGOs. It will also require a more holistic approach to how we value success above and beyond pure economic drivers. It will necessitate relationships with suppliers that are fully transparent and an honest, on-going conversation with the public about what constitutes responsible consumption.

Inspiring consumer behaviour change is going to be one of the hardest tasks the world of marketing, public relations and advertising has ever undertaken. Yet it is also one that the creative and persuasive industries are uniquely suited to and skilled in. After all, any profession that can conjure out of thin air a market for diamonds should find promoting sustainable consumption easy.

How though do you start telling people that overconsumption is unsustainable when most of the advertising budgets for consumer brands are devoted to persuading people to buy more?

Patagonia is one company with an answer. On Black Friday 2011, the aspirational outdoor lifestyle brand ran a full-page advert in *The New York Times* showing a photo of its top-selling R2 fleece sweater with the caption: "Don't Buy This Jacket." It was inspired by what Patagonia identified as a growing consumer backlash post the 2008 global financial crash against rampant consumerism and a shift towards owning fewer products but of greater value.

In a later essay written to accompany the launch of Patagonia's Responsible Economy campaign, Rick Ridgeway, the company's vice-president of environmental affairs, would revisit some of the environmental and social warnings first posed by the early sustainable school known as the Club of Rome, who argued in a 1972 treatise, *The Limits of Growth*, that unfettered economic expansion was the "elephant in the room".

To back up its Don't Buy This Jacket campaign Patagonia entered into a partnership with eBay called Common Threads. Together they launched a special online second-hand store to extend the lifecycle of Patagonia products. Over a 12-month period starting in 2012, more than 38,000 pre-owned Patagonia items of clothing were resold through the storefront.

In 2013 Patagonia launched a new front in its battle against conspicuous consumption with a marketing campaign, Worn Wear, that highlighted the benefits of making clothes last, and repairing them, rather than discarding them. The brand invited customers to share the stories of adventures they have had in Patagonia clothing, highlighting the emotional attachment and value that we feel for clothing that not only lasts but carries us through important life experiences.

As Patagonia CEO Rose Marcario explained:

> As individual consumers, the single best thing we can do for the planet is to keep our stuff in use longer. This simple act of extending the life of our garments through proper care and repair reduces the need to buy more over time – thereby avoiding the CO_2 emissions, waste output and water usage required to build it.[1]

A 2015 *New Yorker* article neatly described Patagonia's ideal worldview:

> There's bad growth, and then there's good growth. An expanding economy driven by ever greater individual consumption of ever more disposable products is bad. In a more sustainable future, people will buy fewer things at higher prices, technological innovation will reduce the impact of those products' manufacture, and the goods themselves will be made to last and then be recycled at the end of their useful lives. Since those are the kinds of products Patagonia is striving to make, and the kinds of relationships to products that Patagonia is trying to foster, then the more that Patagonia expands its market share, the better. The new economy must grow out from beneath the old one.

Given Patagonia's well-documented environmental culture and pedigree, few people doubted the authenticity of its efforts to reduce overall consumption. But, as the *New Yorker* also pointed out, one of the main results of the Don't Buy This Jacket and Worn Wear campaigns was that sales of Patagonia products skyrocketed while only a fraction of those products were repaired or recycled.

So was Patagonia helping or hurting consumer behaviour change? Surely, in the long run, society needs companies like Patagonia that espouse buying fewer and better quality products – especially if their methods and philosophy can also spread to the clothing those who can't afford Patagonia gear will buy.

Lydia Baird, a student at the Fashion Institute of Technology told the *New Yorker*:

> We definitely have to consume less, and there's no way the world is going to be a perfect place. But maybe production can be done better. Maybe production doesn't have to be a bad thing. And maybe Patagonia can lead us there.[2]

Other forward-thinking apparel makers share Patagonia's vision of responsible production and consumption. Levi Strauss created an entire line of WaterLess jeans sold on the principle that it reduced the amount of water used in making each pair (some 1,800 gallons of water) by up to 96 percent.[3] CEO Chip Burgh even went as far as to encourage consumers to stop washing his core product – pointing out at a series of public events in 2014 that nearly half the water usage associated with denim jeans takes place at home due to overwashing.[4]

Perhaps, though, the biggest indicator that responsible fashion consumption had gone mainstream came in 2016 when Swedish apparel retailer H&M – one of the leading "fast fashion" brands – enlisted rapper and fashion icon M.I.A. to create a music video titled *Rewear It* that accompanied its Close the Loop recycling campaign.[5]

Can we change how and what we eat?

The need to change consumer behaviour around fashion, apparel and various resource-heavy consumer goods is pressing. However, it pales against the urgent need to address the way the world grows and consumes food. That task may yet turn out to be the singular most important sustainability struggle of all our lifetimes.

Given food's singular importance for every person on earth, you might think that our modern, sophisticated society would have worked out an equitable system to ensure all humans have both enough to eat and the option and knowledge to choose tasty, nutritious food.

That is not the case. For many people the challenge remains simply finding enough food to eat. For others the issue is getting access to the right mix of food to ensure a healthy diet. For many more the challenge isn't one of availability but of cost: how can they feed themselves and their families on limited economic means? Then there is the rapidly expanding global middle class.

Their most pressing question is: what type of cuisine do I want to eat and do I want to cook it or pay someone else to cook it for me?

The world's population is set to grow dramatically over the next few decades, reaching nearly 10 billion by 2050.[6] To feed all those people we'll need to double global food production and we'll have to change how we grow and produce that food. At the same time, the food industry will have to reshape the often unhealthy consumer attitudes to eating and drinking – attitudes that it has been responsible for shaping in the first place.

Fixing a failing system

The stark reality is that the global food system is already at breaking point. The challenges start with the way we grow our food and the way we manage our land. They continue in the form of millions of people who still lack the right balance of nutrients in their diet. And they are compounded by a modern mainstream consumer culture that has become infatuated with the allure of cheap, convenience food offered by big food producers and, as a result, has lost connection to where food comes from and how it is made.

The development of our modern food system didn't take place in a vacuum; it was a response to the growing demand for food from a rapidly urbanising global society, one that no longer had the time, space, nor inclination to cultivate its own food. What grew out of this demand was a food industry that produces the brands, products and tastes that so many of us love, whether it be those favourite meals of our childhood, the convenience food we snack on or the everyday staples we depend on to help manage our busy lives.

Yet many of the strategies and processes that have been employed to grow, produce, distribute and market food in our modern society place enormous strains on natural resources, biodiversity, the environment and the people charged with producing it.

From an agriculture standpoint the demands of our current food system have ramped up the use of pesticides, herbicides and fertilisers, and they have accelerated the intensive farming of core crops like maize, soya and palm oil (and the deforestation often associated with growing these crops).

Agriculture already uses almost 38 percent of the world's total land surface area while nearly 70 percent of the world's surface water supplies are used for farming. Today it takes between 2,000 to 5,000 litres of water to grow and process the food that we consume each day.[7]

This industrialisation of the land has devastating consequences in terms of soil degradation and erosion. According to the renowned food writer and campaigner, Michael Pollan, "scientists estimate that cultivated soil has lost 50 to 70 percent of its carbon, speeding up climate change."[8]

One of the undoubted achievements of our industrial agricultural complex is its ability to produce large amounts of filling food at a very affordable price. Unfortunately the global food industry has often delivered this success in the form of convenience food that maximises the use of sugars and fats at the expense of more nutritious ingredients. As a result, today millions of people are consuming too many calories – and not necessarily the right calories.

You might expect obesity to be primarily what people now like to call a "first world problem" but worldwide obesity has doubled since 1980 and it is estimated that 13 percent of all adults aged 18 are clinically obese with a further 39 percent being overweight.[9] Increasingly, it is becoming a global disease and one that poses a double burden for many developing nations even as they also struggle with widespread undernourishment.

The fact that something is very wrong with our relationship to food is not lost on the general public. They may not talk in technical terms like resource scarcity, sustainable sourcing, biodiversity or nutrition deficiency but it is beginning to dawn on them that something is very wrong with the way our food is farmed and the way we are consuming it even if they don't yet have a full understanding of the impact that their food decisions are having on the planet.

Over the last decade there has been a marked increase in consumer awareness and appreciation of healthy nutritious food – particularly when it comes to home cooking. One global consumer survey in 2015 found that 66 percent of respondents were willing to pay more for products they considered sustainable, and the type of ingredients that go into making the product and how it is made influenced the decisions of more than half the respondents.[10]

A number of factors have contributed to this growing consumer awareness about food quality and nutrition. Celebrity chefs have played their part, as has the hipster-inspired embrace of artisanal, locally sourced food and the urban and suburban love affair with shopping at farmer's markets and growing our own fruit and vegetables. Even rearing chickens is no longer considered a rural pursuit!

Social media, perhaps, has played the biggest role in making food a topic we all care about. Today a digital publishing army of food bloggers, Facebookers, Instagrammers, Tumblrs, tweeters and YouTubers are celebrating and sharing "food porn" images from restaurants, upmarket street food carts and artisan stores, and they are swapping recipes and tips for home cooking and baking.

Sites all over the world like Food Babe, Eat Like a Girl, The Sugar Free Revolution and Rens Kroes are building on the success of original food blogger Julie Powell (whose writing inspired the movie *Julie and Julia*), Instagram accounts like Food52 have more than a million followers and even "nomnom" – once obscure online slang for tasty food – has entered the popular lexicon.

Of course, social media isn't used simply to celebrate food. Even as today's home cooks want their food to be flavourful and delicious they also have heightened expectations about nutrition and the sustainability of that food. On an almost daily basis, nutritionists, activists and everyday people are shouting their concerns and sharing information (and misinformation) about how our food is grown and prepared.

In recent years social media–driven campaigns by the likes of celebrity chef Jamie Oliver and environmental groups like Greenpeace, as well as grassroots movements led by Mommy Bloggers all over the world, have helped change consumer perceptions and buying habits around issues like battery hens, sustainable sourcing of fish, deforestation and loss of biodiversity related to palm oil production, the nutritional value of school meals and many more. The viral, connected power of social media has fuelled these campaigns and made them resonate on a global scale.

The good news then is that so many consumers understand the food system needs to change. The bad news is that most still don't have enough knowledge or information about our extremely complicated food system to ask the right questions and make sustainable purchasing and lifestyle decisions. For example, they hear about the deforestation problems associated with the palm oil industry and assume all palm oil must be bad. Yet they are unaware of the collaborative work being undertaken to develop sustainable production standards by NGOs, palm oil producers and food companies. In the same way a growing number of consumers rightly demand governments and companies act to reduce greenhouse gases, yet they are unaware of how their own diets (specifically a preference for meat – beef in particular) play a role in climate change.

Without a better consumer understanding of how they can make sustainable food decisions, the growing, social media–fuelled noise around the failing food system will be just that: noise.

Why Big Food needs to change consumer behaviour

The threats posed by resource scarcity, climate change, unsustainable farming and lack of nutrition are going to have a direct impact on the food system in the near future. Traditionally we might have looked to governments and NGOs for environmental and social solutions but, increasingly, it is the major food companies with their large-scale farming, distribution networks and marketing machines that are the best placed to shape a sustainable food system and changing consumer behaviour.

Behind the scenes, collaborative progress is being made in some areas – take the pan-industry initiatives around sustainable palm oil (referenced in Chapter 2) and soy as well as the long-term and on-going collaboration around sustainable agriculture practices being undertaken through organisations like SAI Platform, a food industry umbrella group that was set up to research and promote sustainable agriculture.

Perhaps though the most immediate impact that companies can have is in helping reshape consumer behaviour about food waste, a global problem that touches every part of the food industry. Globally one third of all food is wasted and the direct economic cost of this wasteful behaviour is estimated at

$750 billion annually. Food waste also adds 3.3 billion tonnes of greenhouse gases to the atmosphere.[11]

Inefficient harvesting, storage, transportation and retail selling practices are part of the food waste problem, but consumers also contribute significantly by discarding tonnes upon tonnes of produce labelled past the sell-by date.

Individually, different companies and NGOs already tackle consumer food waste. UK retailer Sainsbury's teamed up with Google to launch the Food Rescue app. It allowed users to input up to nine ingredients via text or voice input and in return they were presented with more than 1,200 choices of recipes. The app recorded the weight of food rescued and the money saved per completed recipe (so the app offers a real financial incentive as well as usefulness), which was then fed into a leader board to show which regions across the United Kingdom were saving the most food. Tech start-up, Olio, also created a free app that connected neighbours with each other and with local businesses so surplus food could be shared rather than discarded.

One of the most striking and successful of consumer waste campaigns started in France with Intermarché's Inglorious Fruits and Vegetables.[12] In 2014, following new EU laws cracking down on food waste, the supermarket ran an advertising campaign celebrating non-perfectly formed fruit and vegetables – like the Ugly Carrot, the Hideous Orange and the Failed Lemon – that supermarkets would normally reject due to their belief that consumers would buy only perfect-looking produce. Because of this perfectionist aesthetic as much as 20 to 40 percent of fresh produce is wasted, according to the United Nations Environment Programme.[13]

The campaign was a national sensation that resulted in Intermarché's store traffic increasing by 24 percent and sales of fruits and vegetables by 10 percent. Indeed, Inglorious Fruits and Vegetables was such a hit that it was mimicked by other retailers across Europe, the United States and even New Zealand.[14]

Sustainable growing practices, labour conditions and quality of ingredients are other areas where companies can help shift consumer behaviour. Food companies have long worked with third-party sustainable production certification organisations like Fairtrade and Rainforest Alliance to demonstrate to consumers that their sourcing and supply chains benefit the well-being of the farmers who produce the food as well as deliver nutritious and good-tasting food.

Rainforest Alliance was responsible for one of the most creative awareness-raising campaigns of the past decade in the form of Follow the Frog. It was fronted by a funny video parodying the extents that some over-the-top do-gooders will go to be "green" – a "truly brilliant example of short-form advocacy filmmaking", in the words of cultural zeitgeist blog Boing.[15]

Still, though, a great deal of confusion remains around ethical labelling. Consumers often assume that sustainably certified products are going to cost more (even though that isn't necessarily the case). They also are confused by food labelling – ostensibly a way for producers to offer a transparent explanation of the ingredients used to make the food we buy. Too often the information just adds to the confusion and suspicion felt by consumers. It will continue to do so until food companies work together to create consistent labelling standards on sourcing and nutrition, and to educate consumers on how to make responsible food choices.

Some are starting to just that. General Mills has started to remove artificial flavours and colours from artificial sources from its cereals as well as offering a gluten-free version of the Cheerio brand while Campbell Soup Company took the unprecedented step of informing consumers when any of their products includes genetically modified ingredients (see Q&A with Campbell's chief sustainability officer, Dave Stangis).

Promoting the fact that you're removing artificial ingredients can be a tricky message to convey after you have spent the past decades telling consumers your products were the best they could be. General Mills took the approach of appealing to parents' desire to do the best for their kids. Its Parent Promises campaign highlighted that General Mills was on the side of parents and pledged to do the best for kids by removing artificial additives.

Kraft Heinz took a different approach in 2015 when it relaunched its iconic Kraft Mac & Cheese with a new formula that got rid of artificial preservatives and artificial dyes and replaced them with paprika, annatto and turmeric. The changes were in response to consumer unease about artificial ingredients but still Kraft was uneasy about how consumers would react.

When the reformulated version was first released, the company said nothing about the changes. In fact, it was only after Kraft had sold 50 million boxes of the new product that it created an advertising campaign featuring TV host Craig Kilborn explaining how it had hoodwinked the public. As Greg Guidotti, Kraft's vice president for meal solutions, told *The New York Times*, when the brand announced in early 2015 that it would change the ingredients, people started complaining through social media that the mac and cheese would taste different. "We knew we wanted to address that tension," Guidotti said.[16]

Two years after Kraft made the switch people were still complaining on Facebook that the old artificial version tasted better – a cautionary lesson for all brands that unless their healthier product is also superior it will fail to connect with the public.

That's a problem food companies will increasingly have to tackle as they create new products that can balance the need to satisfy consumer tastes with the growing concerns about the sustainability of our food system.

Beyond beef . . . and pork and poultry

At the heart of food system problem is consumer demand for proteins and how we obtain them. Proteins are among the primary and essential building blocks of our bodies. They help create bone, cartilage, hair, muscle and other body tissues. We can get different types of proteins from various sources. The majority of the people on this planet, however, like to get their proteins from animal meat, be it beef, pork, poultry or fish. Unfortunately, this collective appetite for meat poses a threat to our ability to feed ourselves in the years to come.

Consider the facts. The livestock we rear for food and dairy uses nearly 30 percent of the world's ice-free landmass and produces 14.5 percent of all greenhouse gas emissions, according to United Nations' research. Raising animals also requires enormous amounts of food: it takes at least 7 kilograms of grain to produce 1 kilograms of beef, 5 kilograms for pork and 2.5 kilograms for poultry. Then there is the drain on water resources: 12,000 gallons are needed to produce just one pound of beef. No wonder then that nearly 50 percent of the water used each year in the United States is directed to raising animals.

As the world's population continues to grow so will the number of meat eaters, especially in emerging nations where eating more meat is associated with increased prosperity. Beef sales in China alone have risen 19,000 percent in the past decade.[17]

With the world on a food collision course the only sustainable path is to reduce the amount of meat we consume. With that goal in mind a growing number of nutrition experts and food companies (including some meat producers) advocate a radical rebalance of how we get our protein. The solution, they believe, is to replace meat with so-called green protein in the form of plants.

Making the shift away from animal protein to plants makes sense in terms of personal health. The recommended dietary allowance of protein is just 0.8 grams of protein per kilogram of body weight each day – an amount that can be easily obtained through plant sources such as peas, sorghum, mushrooms and soybeans. It's true that plant protein doesn't deliver the same the same composition of complete amino acids as animal protein, but it offers other health benefits and advantages over meat – lower risks of cholesterol and heart disease, for example – as the estimated 375 million vegetarians around the world can attest.

But just because eating vegetables makes scientific, dietary and sustainable sense this is not enough to make the meat eaters of the world give up. What role then can plants and vegetables play in feeding a world that has come to put animal protein on a pedestal?

Michael Pollan neatly encapsulated a sustainable approach to eating when he wrote "Eat food, not too much, mostly plants" in his book, *Food Rules: An Eater's Manual*.[18] For that mantra to become a global reality, companies will have to create new types of plant-based food choices that will be just as tasty and appealing as a juicy hamburger, succulent lamb chops or even crispy bacon!

Green protein's potential to disrupt and transform the food industry has already attracted a great deal of interest from the technology community of Silicon Valley with food start-ups like Beyond Meat, Impossible Foods and Califia Farms attracting significant investment from venture capital, other tech companies and even major meat producers. Their motivation is financial, not culinary, of course.

As Ali Partovi, a San Francisco investor in past successes such as Dropbox and Airbnb, told the *Economist*:

> Anytime you can find a way to use plant protein instead of animal protein there's an enormous efficiency in terms of the energy, water and all sorts of other inputs involved – which translates at the end of the day to saving money.[19]

As every Silicon Valley entrepreneur knows, though, even the most brilliant new technology will fail if it doesn't capture the public's imagination. For green protein to really challenge animal protein, food companies will have to persuade consumers of its appeal over and above the traditional "green is good" argument. Producing a superior product will be crucial – few consumers will swap animal meat for plant protein if it doesn't taste as good – as will the marketing, branding and communication of the plant-based meat products.

That might sound like a daunting challenge for the marketers of the world, but latent demand for plant proteins already exists just waiting to be tapped. While just 7.3 million Americans are vegetarians, more than 22 million consider themselves Flexitarians who eat mainly vegetables and occasionally meat. According to the US Department of Agriculture, annual meat consumption has fallen by 15 percent in the last decade and 33 percent since the 1970s. Eating trends in Europe mirror the United States.[20]

Enduring cultural and religious norms can also play an important role in reducing animal protein consumption, especially in parts of Asia such as India where 31 percent of the population is vegetarian. That means there's a ready-made market for new vegetarian-based food products that build on Asia's cultural and culinary heritage.

Fifty years ago, families in the western world ate five times less meat than we do today. So, in the big picture of food history, our current meat fixation is just a minor footnote. However, if we continue consuming meat at the same rate as the last 50 years, that footnote could turn into the event that alters the history of human civilisation. How we can transition in the most efficient and tasty way from animal to plant protein should be food for thought for producers and consumers alike.

Q&A with Dave Stangis, vice president of corporate responsibility and chief sustainability officer for Campbell Soup Company

Q: What are the major sustainability issues Campbell's faces?

A: Our sustainability priorities are fairly consistent across the food and beverage sector. In addition to responsible sourcing and sustainable agriculture, we are also seeking to drive measurable social impact in the communities in which we work. At Campbell, our Healthy Communities programme is now in place at four different Campbell locations and seeks to measurably improve the health of young people with a focus on childhood hunger and obesity. Going forward, I would say that transparency and traceability are the two key drivers of the next version of sustainability in our sector.

Q: Have these issues grown/changed over the last decade?

A: Technology and consumer trends in the food business have rapidly accelerated over the last decade. Many of the trends that we identify as positive disruptions in the food sector are simply the advancing technology. This technology plays out in many ways ranging from Big Data tools in agriculture to the Internet of Things and consumer's interests in designing diets and lifestyles to achieve their health and nutrition needs. Those major technology trends coupled with tremendous shifts in demographics are what is driving sustainability today in our sector.

Q: Can you give a little more detail about the way technology is driving change?

A: Technology is both enabling new methods throughout the food supply chain and driving new levels and desires for transparency among consumers. Just about everything you can imagine wanting to be able to do in the food and beverage supply chain is now technically feasible. Tracing ingredients to their source is a matter of technology, time and investment. Consumers have the ability now (or will so soon) to assess the nutritional profile of just about any product as well as its provenance. The era of personalised nutrition and 100 percent online food shopping is just around the corner.

Q: In this new social age, what do real people want when it comes to feeding their families and themselves?

A: Consumers still want the same thing from the food they eat and serve to their families as they always have. Primarily they want to trust the food and the food supply. Food safety reigns above all. Beyond that, consumers have grown wary of too much innovation in their food. While consumers are looking for new tastes and formats, they are increasingly looking for fresher choices made with ingredients they know and understand. They want to believe that their food choices are good for them and for the planet. They want to purchase from companies whose values match their own. And on top of that, they do not want to make any sacrifices in terms of cost, taste or convenience.

Q: Does sustainability figure into their thinking (even if they don't use the word "sustainability")?

A: Consumers do use the word "sustainability". They often don't know exactly what the word entails across the food supply chain – or for that matter across any complex value chains. However, they do understand that sustainably produced translates to trust, and that sustainably produced means that it is good or at least neutral to the earth and their community. The most important take away with respect to food is that consumers use the concepts of sustainable as a proxy for good or healthy. Many if not most consumers feel that food that is sustainably produced is better for them and their family.

Q: Do consumers need better information in order to understand the complexities of the food system and nutrition? And what role can companies play in better informing and educating consumers?

A: This is an interesting question. It is hard to say what consumers actually need. Some consumers would say they have too much information already and that information complicates the decision-making when it comes to food for themselves and their family. Many consumers want more information about their food and where it comes from because they believe it helps them make better decisions. They also believe, and rightly so, that transparency builds trust. And that trust is what they ultimately seek. I believe food companies and all companies in the food value chain from farm to fork have a role to play in informing consumers. I think most companies can do a better job at sharing the story of their food, how it's grown or raised, how it's produced, how it's packaged, and the benefits it can provide from a health and nutrition standpoint. We all have a role in this regard and I think we all have more to do.

Q: What is Campbell's doing in terms of sustainability communication that meets the changing needs and demands of consumers?

A: Campbell's purpose and real food philosophy are helping drive our narrative around all of our products and ingredients. This extends to the choices we make around the ingredients we use, the way they are sourced and our goals with respect to sustainability during production. Campbell has two Public Benefit Corporations within its own company – Plum Organics and the Soulfull Project – that are anchored in our mission and live and breathe those values with consumers. Beyond that, the enterprise narrative has changed significantly in the past three to four years to embrace transparency. The other key angle to keep in mind is the change in internal and employee communications. We have recently launched a new set of employee values that bridge to the company purpose and the real food philosophy that embrace a new entrepreneurial spirit, accountability and tolerance for risk taking.

Q: What will consumers be most interested in/concerned about in terms of food over the next decade? Can companies provide leadership on these issues now?

A: I would suggest that we will see increasing attention to the role of food and agriculture in the global climate change debate. I also believe that the march to transparency and traceability within the agricultural supply chain will identify new challenges and opportunities for companies with respect to consumer expectations. One example of a topic that has just exploded in the last few years is food waste. Most scientists and consumers know that we waste too much food on the planet. Companies, governments and start-ups have all taken a new look at food waste and what can be done to solve the challenge in light of new technology coming to bear and transparency in the marketplace. This is just one example of what you see evolve in the sector as time marches on. Companies are taking leadership in the food waste agenda and I suspect you see them take new leadership in the broader sustainability and health and wellness agenda as well.

Q: Finally, to tackle the many challenges they face, food companies will surely have to work together to change the system. Is that happening?

A: The new trends that we are seeing in our sector have to do with cross-company and cross-sector collaboration. We are seeing much more partnership on these topics between manufacturers such as Campbell and retail partners. There is broad alignment in the sector on major topics such as deforestation and climate change, health and nutrition, sustainable agriculture, and forced labour.

Notes

1 https://www.patagonia.com/blog/2015/11/repair-is-a-radical-act/
2 www.newyorker.com/business/currency/patagonias-anti-growth-strategy
3 www.sustainablebrands.com/news_and_views/waste_not/jennifer_elks/levis_waterless_jeans_have_saved_770_million_liters_so_far
4 http://levistrauss.com/unzipped-blog/2014/05/stop-washing-your-jeans-lsco-ceo-chip-bergh-talks-sustainability-at-fortunes-brainstorm-green-conference/

5   www.marketingweek.com/2016/04/12/hm-aims-to-make-recycling-cool-with-first-ever-sustainability-campaign/

6   https://www.theguardian.com/global-development/2015/jul/29/un-world-population-prospects-the-2015-revision-9-7-billion-2050-fertility

7   http://www.fao.org/nr/water/aquastat/didyouknow/index3.stm

8   www.washingtonpost.com/opinions/2015/12/04/fe22879e-990b-11e5-8917-653b65c809eb_story.html?utm_term=.ee98a8e70660

9   http://www.who.int/mediacentre/factsheets/fs311/en/

10 http://www.nielsen.com/uk/en/insights/news/2015/green-generation-millennials-say-sustainability-is-a-shopping-priority.html

11 Lucas Simons *Changing the Food Game: Market Transformation Strategies for Sustainable Agriculture*. London: Greenleaf Publishing, Routledge, 2017

12 www.dandad.org/awards/professional/2015/direct/24619/inglorious-fruits-and-vegetables/

13 http://www.fao.org/save-food/resources/keyfindings/en/

14 www.npr.org/sections/thesalt/2014/12/09/369613561/in-europe-ugly-sells-in-the-produce-aisle

15 http://boingboing.net/2012/10/24/an-epic-nonprofit-psa-follo.html

16 www.nytimes.com/2016/03/21/business/media/kraft-reveals-revamped-mac-and-cheese-50-million-boxes-later.html?ref=business&_r=0

17 https://www.bloomberg.com/graphics/2017-feeding-china/

18 Michael Pollan *Food Rules: An Eater's Manual*. Penguin Books. 2009

19 https://gbr.economist.com/articles/view/5518bdb780cac48b49afdc5b

20 http://fortune.com/2015/10/27/red-meat-consumption-decline/

Part 3

The know-how

Chapter 9

How to show, not tell

The era of telling the public how good a company is and expecting those messages to be embraced at face value is well and truly over. Consumers have access to so much information in real time nowadays that only those companies that back up their words with actions will win respect.

How companies demonstrate and communicate their commitments to community, environment and greater society will go a long way to winning that respect. As we've seen in Part 2, those commitments include smart collaboration with peers, competitors and even antagonists. They involve strong leadership and a dedication to being transparent. And they include a drive to educate, empower, innovate and inspire behaviour change as they anticipate and plan for a world where products and services will need to be more sustainable.

Who is your community and what does it care about?

As the Internet grew in importance during the late 1990s commentators liked to refer to it as the "Information Superhighway" – a fast-moving yet structured method of communicating dominated by a minority of organisations and corporate entities that had the funds and technological ability to build and maintain a presence on the web.

Social media, offering anyone the power to publish their thoughts and opinions, is less a monolithic superhighway and more a network of online byroads and country lanes.

Because of this disintermediated digital infrastructure, the relevant communities that sustainability communicators want to talk with tend to be completely separate and yet connected at the same time.

This complex relationship is applicable both on a general audience and issue-based level. Gone are the days when information for employees could be packaged and directed solely to this group. Today, employees will share their ideas about their sustainability work with their friends via social media and in many cases they are encouraged to do so by their employers – though those same employers seem far less keen on social media sharing when the company gets something wrong.

Information that once would have been interesting only to sustainability trade media now can be found and shared on thousands of dedicated sustainability blogs, Twitter accounts and LinkedIn pages. And, as we've seen in Chapter 2, NGO news and activism that might once have reached just a small group of concerned citizens now quickly grabs the attention of mainstream media organisations because they are constantly monitoring social media conversation trends for the next big story – and vice versa.

Indeed, the relationship between mainstream media and social media is so symbiotic at this point that it's impossible to compartmentalise target audiences in the way content planners might have in the past.

If there *is* a way of compartmentalising sustainability content and information it is by specific topic. Information about solar power will have a very specific audience, as will updates about sustainable agriculture or socially responsible investing (SRI). The audience for this content will be narrow given its specific focus but will also be deep given the numbers of people now sharing information on these topic. At the same time some sustainability issues transcend any one sector. Diversity, gender equality and wage parity – to name a few – appeal to a broader group of people across business even though the topic itself might be quite specific.

It's all about the right audience

Facebook has 2 billion active users,[1] Instagram 800 million,[2] Twitter 328 million,[3] and Snapchat 166 million.[4] So social media is all about the size of audience – right?

That's the myth that has developed in recent years as the advertising and public relations world has come to dominate brand interaction on social media. You can see why advertisers, media buyers and public relations experts would want to create this view of social media: it corresponds perfectly with the type of big-campaign mentality that so many of them are structured to deliver. More views and more shares equals more reach – that holy grail of digital media measurement – so it's no wonder that whole new mini-sectors of AdTech have sprung up in recent years to run marketing on Facebook while online influencer marketing has become a must-have skill for any digital public relations firm.

The reality of social media sustainability communication is very different, however. Companies intent on demonstrating authenticity and nurturing community have to focus on the *quality* of engagement rather than quantity. So, while the power and connected community of so-called influencers can certainly help, successful social media sustainability communication depends on identifying the right audience rather than the biggest one.

Who are the voices that your community most respects? Who are your biggest constructive critics? Who will give you an honest evaluation that can improve sustainability in the company?

These are the voices you need to listen to and partner with. Win them over to your sustainability credentials and you'll be amazed how quickly the message spreads through that interconnected network of mutual interests.

What have you got to say that is relevant to your community and how should you say it?

Once companies have identified the right audience to talk with, then they need to have something to show them. Talking about 2025 sustainability goals isn't going to cut it. Sometimes the reason why companies talk about aspirations rather than showing real work is because they aren't doing anything worth talking about. Obviously those companies have to stop trying to run when they are still learning to walk. Many more companies, however, are doing solid and sometimes inspiring sustainability work. It's just that the communications departments don't know about it.

All too often the sort of sustainability stories that would convince sceptics and build respect both inside and outside the organisation are buried deep in research and development, supplier relationships or operations and logistics. How often does the communication or marketing team ever get to talk to their colleagues deep in the business?

Think like an editor

To unearth the sustainability stories that will win respect and regain trust communicators need to start thinking like an editor would at a newspaper or magazine and start treating the organisation as a "beat". What is going on in your company in terms of sustainability? Where are the great stories and who is doing the great work? Digging deep in this way will uncover the voices and stories that give credibility to sustainability strategy and communications. But be prepared. Digging like an editor or reporter will also uncover aspects of the organisation that might not be so complimentary.

This is where in-house journalistic reporting really earns its stripes. If communicators can highlight areas of the company that need to be improved or where sustainability standards are slipping, there's a decent chance of addressing the problems before some pesky NGO starts digging around or before an employee starts complaining on social media. Because of its importance in portraying trust and respect, sustainability has to be the conscience of the organisation. Having communication teams who think like an editor will help keep the entire company honest and consistent to the goals it wants to aspire to.

How companies tell their story consistently and with authenticity

These next sections look at the various written and visual techniques that companies and brands are using to good effect to communicate sustainability.

Blogs and social media magazines

Blogging may have faded in popularity since its heyday in the early 2000s, but this longer form of social media publishing remains a powerful and useful tool for sustainability communicators.

Part of the reason is that most sustainability stories have a strong narrative element to them or warrant a deep explanation of the science and thinking that drives the sustainability activity. It's also true that a lot of good sustainability stories don't necessarily lend themselves to traditional marketing and advertising campaigns.

In the past these stories might have ended up packaged as a press release along with all the rest of the corporate news detritus that no-one ever reads. Instead, a number of companies and brands have embraced blogging and online magazines to bring sustainability stories to life and present them in a way that is readable and accessible by various social media audiences.

The audience for sustainability blogging appears to be quite mixed judging from the content and approach taken by companies. On the one hand there is an obvious kindred spirit audience of sustainability professionals who will be interested in sustainability content no matter how it is packaged. On the other hand, social media opened up new audience possibilities and blogs like Timberland's Bootmaker showed it was possible both to appeal to the sustainability community and also to customers with stories that highlighted the outdoor brand's "Earthkeeping" environmental commitment. In the early days of the blog, back in 2009, Timberland's sustainability story was often told by its founder and then-CEO Jeff Schwartz. He stopped writing when he sold Timberland to VF Corporation in 2011 but the blog continued.

Intel's corporate social responsibility blog maintained a tighter focus – informing more traditional sustainability stakeholders of the work it was doing in the areas of recycling and community development. Other companies have persevered with dedicated sustainability blogs in the past decade including Danone, Dell and even ExxonMobil though, in the past, it used its voice to question scientific consensus on climate change![5]

A few companies, however, saw the opportunity to completely reinvent their approach to corporate and sustainability communications by fully embracing a "magazine mentality".

One of the early sustainability blog/magazines was the German insurance company Allianz. It launched a sustainability-focused online magazine in 2010 called Knowledge. This shared expertise on climate change and other sustainability issues and it developed an on-going conversation with relevant communities.

Knowledge became the go-to destination for anyone wanting to stay on top of climate change, energy and human impact thinking (key areas of business for Allianz) and was one of the first sustainability-focused sites to employ a social media "satellite system". The core content and thinking was published direct to the Knowledge microsite, then shared where relevant through its social spokes on Facebook, Twitter, YouTube, Slideshare and Google+.

What Knowledge lacked in panache and editorial style it more than made up for with the quality of its thinking and breadth of topics. Today, its authority and repository of sustainability thinking would be more useful than ever. Unfortunately Allianz discontinued Knowledge in 2015.

Coca-Cola Inc. also saw the potential in reshaping what once would have been corporate stories for a more diverse social media audience. Coca-Cola's Unbottled online magazine featured a dedicated sustainability section that elevated sustainability out of the depths of stakeholder relations into the spotlight of corporate brand communication. Levi Strauss employed a similar approach. Its Unzipped blog on its corporate site highlights sustainable production, sourcing and community projects.

As mentioned in Chapter 6 Unilever created a dedicated sustainability content hub called Project Sunlight and used it both as a badge of pride – tallying every visitor to the site as a vindication of its commitment to sustainable living and consumption – and as a way of cataloguing and showcasing the sustainability campaign work being done by its many brands.

But, among all the companies employing a social media magazine approach one stands out above the rest.

Over the past decade GE excelled at creating shareable content for the social media age – not least its smart use of blogs and online magazines for storytelling.

Take Txchnologist, an online magazine that GE sponsors, but does not exert editorial control over. It offers an optimistic take on the future and humanity's ability to tackle the big challenges of our era through industry, technology and ingenuity. Being one step removed from GE, it can provide a broader look at the world of science and technology, covering topics such as Earth, Space, Materials, Energy, Life and Nature, Building, Transportation and Computing.

Another online magazine, Ideas Lab, provides a platform to explore how new ideas, innovations and public policies will transform business, industry and the global economy. More than 170 thought leaders from across industry, government, academia and non-profit communities contributed to Ideas Lab in recent years.

The engine room of GE's editorial output has been GE Reports – a daily online corporate magazine that features stories about innovation, science and technology, as well as viewpoints on topics of relevance to GE and the wider world.

GE's entire social media publishing approach satisfies a number of needs. First, it creates an agile marketing approach that allows this massive corporation to highlight many elements of its operations in creative ways that it simply couldn't achieve with traditional TV and print advertising. Second – and this is key for a company that employs more than 300,000 people and is always on the lookout for new talent – keeping near constant communication flowing through Snapchat, Instagram and Tumblr helps the company stay relevant to a new generation of future employees.

Whatever platform GE publishes on, each piece of content aims to put a different lens on GE's work. As GE CMO Linda Boff explained to *Marketing Week*,

> We try to find ways to bring it to life, to tell that story in fresh, unexpected, human and relatable ways that don't diminish the fact that we're working on things like bringing electricity to a billion people around the world.[6]

Content marketing and native advertising

One of social media's greatest impacts over the past decade has been to accelerate the demise of traditional newspaper and magazine publishing models. The public's expectation that online content should be free (encouraged it has to be said by the majority of news publishers) combined with the ability to share content via social media acted like a time bomb on hard-copy sales of newspapers in particular. With digital advertising delivering just a fraction of the revenue publishers receive from print news, media organisations have been forced to embrace new business models, among which native advertising/ content marketing has proven very successful.

Advertising, marketing and public relations agencies have jumped into the content marketing game by establishing agency content shops and studios to create the type of online storytelling (often in video form) that can fit seamlessly into the digital pages of newspapers and magazines without screaming "Advertising!" at the reader.

It's fair to say that many old-school journalists remain sceptical about the long-term impact that native advertising will have on news organisations' credibility. Too often, branded content sits a little too cosily next to news and features, while the disclosures that the content is paid for by the sponsors can easily be overlooked by readers who don't expect to find advertising in their news stream.

That said, native advertising can be executed in a manner that preserves the credibility of the news organisation while offering the sponsor the "thought leadership" it desires. In 2014 *The New York Times*' in-house T Brand content studio created an impressive 1,500 word investigation of prison conditions as a piece of native advertising for Showtime's *Orange Is the New Black* prison drama.[7]

Sustainability communicators have also embraced native advertising. Bank of America partnered with *Quartz* in 2015 to produce infographics around climate change in the run up to the Paris climate change talks. Unilever, for its part, partnered with the *Guardian* to create Live Better, a native advertising channel designed to promote sustainable consumer behaviour, and it also worked with Upworthy to sponsor consumer-focused feel-good sustainability content.

In other cases brands have used native advertising as a way to augment larger sustainability campaigns. Philips partnered with the *Daily Telegraph* in the United Kingdom for its 100 Days of Innovation campaign. The *Telegraph* highlighted an innovation each day for 100 days through daily posts on a dedicated microsite.

Native advertising with the *Telegraph* also helped Kenco's Coffee vs Gangs campaign reach a mainstream audience that may not have connected with the campaign via Facebook or Twitter. Coffee vs Gangs was a sustainability initiative that offered a group of vulnerable young people in Honduras a way to escape rampant gang culture by training them to become coffee farmers. The campaign was part of a larger Coffee Made Happy programme, run by Kenco's parent company, Mondelez, which pledged a $200 million investment in 1 million coffee farming entrepreneurs by 2020.[8]

Coffee vs Gangs chronicled the highs and lows of 20 young people who agreed to take part in the 11-month training scheme. It was told through blog posts and videos that sought to establish the authenticity of Kenco's ethical programme by "charting the trials and tribulations of the 20 young people as they work with Kenco to develop their business ideas," as *Marketing Week* described the campaign.[9]

The native advertising element played an important role in what Mondelez terms "Storytelling at Scale" – a strategy that encourages marketers to treat social media more like a broadcast channel by balancing paid and earned media. The content on the *Telegraph*'s website pushed viewers back to Facebook, where they could explore more of the brand's campaign posts.[10]

Documentary filmmaking

In recent years marketers have increasingly turned to documentary storytelling to cut through the growing and deafening social media noise to tap into a growing consumer demand for content that isn't simply a throwaway video snack.

Documentary storytelling has become the gold standard of native advertising and content marketing, helping to give companies an authoritative and authentic voice through a medium that commands respect due to its highbrow heritage. But that credibility is only as strong as the story being told, so it's no surprise that some of the most powerful corporate documentaries being made are about sustainability and corporate social responsibility issues.

Some companies turn to documentaries to offer a rich depiction of the sustainability and social impact work they are doing around the world. Siemens took this approach with its *Answers* series of short documentaries that were shot by professional filmmakers and showed how the company's engineering technology was helping communities in places like Nepal and Morocco.

Others look to highlight the work of their suppliers. Italian coffee maker Illy commissioned a professional filmmaker (in this case Lesley Chilcott, director of *An Inconvenient Truth* and *Waiting for Superman*) to make *A Small Section of the World*, the story of a female-run coffee collective in Costa Rica.

Levi Strauss has made documentaries to highlight its commitment to the global skateboarding scene. In a series of short films, the brand travelled to South Africa, Bolivia and India, as well as Oakland, California and the Pine Ridge Reservation in South Dakota where, in partnership with local skate crews and companies, it built skate parks for people who would otherwise never know the freedom of cruising, carving and ollying.

AT&T, perhaps, has the most famous filmmaker collaboration. As mentioned in Chapter 6 it teamed up with renowned director Werner Herzog to create an emotionally wrenching documentary about the perils of texting while driving as part of its long-running It Can Wait campaign.

But no company has used the medium of film/video to shape its sustainability identity better than Patagonia. The privately held outdoor apparel company has always had an editorial mentality – its annual catalogue has long featured storytelling as its principal form of marketing. With films like *DamNation, Jumbo Wild* and *Crude Awakening* the company took those storytelling skills into filmmaking and shone a spotlight on sustainability issues like off-shore oil drilling, the environmental impact of sourcing clean water and tourism overdevelopment.[11]

This storytelling approach also allows Patagonia to stand up for the little guy by communicating issues through the lens of local communities most affected by them in an approach it calls "New Localism".

As Patagonia's Campaigns and Advocacy Director Hans Cole explained to *Fast Company*:

> The New Localism model, where we look at film and the voices of local activists and athletes, our people and community, has really enabled us to have a good technique for getting active around issues and nimble in a different sort of way.[12]

This activist approach to sustainability marketing involves many parts of the business. As Cole explained in the interview,

> There's someone like me, with people from our marketing team who have expertise in storytelling, and our executives, we put heads together, react to what's going on and think about a strategy that's

going to get our employees involved, but also our customers and the wider community.

Virtual and augmented reality

Imagine a day where you're stuck in traffic on that interminable commute to work. Suddenly, the car in front of you begins to lift off the ground, slowly disappearing up into the sky before your very eyes. You turn around to look out of the side and back windows and the same thing is happening – cars everywhere are floating away into the skies.

Or maybe you find yourself caught up in an emergency on a North Sea gas platform. The alarms are sounding to evacuate and you can see flames shooting up around you. You've been told the evacuation instructions, but can you remember how to get out before the platform explodes?

These aren't dream sequences. They are both scenes from virtual reality learning and development experiences created to educate energy employees about climate change and oil and gas workers about safety procedures.[13]

The gaming industry has been talking up the power of virtual reality for more than two decades, but the early technology pioneered by the likes of Sega and Nintendo was clunky, slow and not very convincing as an immersive viewing experience. It wasn't until the arrival of Oculus Rift (and, more importantly, its acquisition by Facebook for $2 billion in 2014) that virtual reality's potential began to be realised – and not in the traditional video gaming ways you might imagine.

Virtual reality is changing people's perception of what can be delivered in terms of visual experiences for all manner of situations. With the arrival of competitors to Oculus Rift in the form of Microsoft's Hololens, Samsung's Gear VR and HTC's Vive, virtual reality seems to have reached a critical mass that will move the technology from the experimental into the mainstream.

Many consumer brands now employ virtual reality to deliver experiential marketing either at exhibitions or for in-store promotions. Yet virtual reality's potential for companies is much bigger than cool brand marketing. A growing number of companies are applying virtual reality storytelling to areas of the business such as employee engagement, learning and development, research and sustainability.

Climate change is one area where virtual reality can be particularly powerful. After all, virtual reality's real power lies not just in showing what is real right now but in opening people's eyes to what could be possible in the future. Academic researchers at Stanford University have been using virtual reality to visualise ocean acidification and its impact on coral reefs.[14] In another example from academia, the University of Southern California sponsored the installation of a virtual reality viewer on Santa Monica Pier in California. It offered a 180-degree view of the shoreline with differing scenarios of flooding by the end of the century.

Even more ambitious was the virtual reality film created to document the construction of Africa's Great Green Wall – a bold project to grow an 8,000km natural wonder of the world across the entire width of Africa. The film (which like many virtual reality experiences was also shared as a 360-degree video on YouTube) shows how the Africa-led project aims to provide food and jobs for the millions of people who live in the Sahel region at the southern edge of the Sahara desert – an area already on the frontline of climate change.[15]

In other instances virtual reality has been used to transport people to places they physically can't visit at present. In 2016 Lockheed Martin launched its Field Trip to Mars – a group virtual reality experience that took schoolchildren on a virtual tour of Mars inside a real school bus. When the children looked out of the windows they experienced the Martian landscape instead of the Washington, DC streets that the bus was actually traversing.[16]

Other virtual reality brand applications are more down to earth. Diageo created a cautionary and shocking drink-and-drive experience depicting how the lives of three sets of passengers are affected after one of the drivers (drunk, of course) causes a multi-vehicle crash.[17] The experience could also be experienced on Facebook, YouTube and a virtual reality app available from *The New York Times*.

Diageo was already committing 20 percent of its broadcast advertising to responsible drinking messages, but, as Diageo's senior vice president for partnerships and entertainment marketing, Dan Sanborn, told *USA Today*: "We feel this [virtual reality experience] is the next evolution of that. . . . If it even changes one person's opinion before getting in a car [drunk] it's a victory for us."[18]

AT&T, for its part, created a similar virtual reality experience for the It Can Wait texting and driving movement.

With virtual reality expected to be a $25 billion industry by 2021, the potential for virtual reality to project a sustainable future is bound to grow. Companies like HTC already see that potential. In early 2017 the virtual reality hardware company launched a $10 million virtual reality fund for content and technologies that will support the UN Sustainable Development Goals.[19]

Notes

1 https://techcrunch.com/2017/06/27/facebook-2-billion-users/
2 https://www.cnbc.com/2017/09/25/how-many-users-does-instagram-have-now-800-million.html
3 www.statista.com/statistics/282087/number-of-monthly-active-twitter-users/
4 https://techcrunch.com/2017/05/10/snapchat-user-count/
5 http://blog.ucsusa.org/gretchen-goldman/still-disinforming-exxonmobils-continued-culpability-in-climate-denial
6 www.marketingweek.com/2017/01/11/general-electric-cmo-redefining-marketing/
7 http://adage.com/article/media/york-times-runs-native-ad-orange-black/293713/

8   www.campaignlive.co.uk/article/why-kenco-taking-gang-culture/1307805#iPzsd5WJ
W4HzM45Z.99

9   https://www.marketingweek.com/2014/08/13/kenco-touts-ethical-credentials-
with-revamped-strategy/

10 www.marketingweek.com/2014/08/13/kenco-touts-ethical-credentials-with-revamped-
strategy/

11 www.fastcompany.com/3038557/the-purpose-driven-marketer-how-patagonia-uses-
storytelling-to-turn-consume

12 www.fastcompany.com/3052442/what-patagonia-learned-so-far-from-mixing-content-
strategy-and-activism

13 The first virtual reality experience was created and scripted by myself for an energy utility
client.

14 http://otherworldinteractive.com/project-view/share-the-science-climate-change/

15 www.greatgreenwall.org/

16 www.adweek.com/brand-marketing/inside-field-trip-mars-single-most-awarded-campaign-
cannes-2016-172531/

17 www.youtube.com/watch?v=jIuwTvtDdVg&feature=youtu.be

18 www.usatoday.com/story/tech/columnist/baig/2016/11/17/die-drunk-driving-accident-
via-terrifying-vr-experience/93984932/

19 https://venturebeat.com/2017/01/18/htc-launches-10-million-vr-fund-to-promote-the-
planets-sustainability/

Chapter 10

The social network effect

All social media networks have one thing in common: strip away the trendy names and minimalist logos, and what you're left with is a powerful, democratised publishing platform.

Some networks like the now-defunct MySpace were established with a specific theme – music – in mind. The content and themes of most other networks are shaped by their users, however.

Over the years brands and companies have adapted their own storytelling to the interests of the community so that YouTube has become a powerhouse platform for the entertainment industry, Vevo the go-to network for musicians and record labels, Pinterest and Instagram virtual shop windows for fashion and retail brands, and LinkedIn a destination for professional services and legions of consultants to share their "expertise".

Here is how some of the world biggest brands have approached sustainability communications through social networks.

Facebook

Ever since Coca-Cola marvelled at the growth of a fan-operated Facebook page devoted to its leading brand and took it over as a vehicle for social media engagement, all other major brands have flocked to the world's most powerful social network.

In less than a decade, those brands have attracted millions of followers and employed hundreds of campaigns to help market their products through the Facebook ecosystem.

You would think then that sustainability focused companies and brands would identify Facebook as a crucial platform for sustainability communications.

You'd be wrong. While many companies use Facebook to talk about corporate social responsibility initiatives – often in the form of highlighting charitable work employees undertake in the community – very few back up the commitments they make on their corporate websites with real Facebook engagement.

This is an incredible opportunity lost given the power brands wield on the platform. To give a sense of how badly Facebook is neglected for sustainability awareness building, from 2014 to 2016, communication consultancy Sustainly researched the Facebook pages of 165 major brands owned by 15 of the world's biggest consumer-goods companies, including Coca-Cola, Danone, Diageo, General Mills, Johnson & Johnson, PepsiCo, P&G and Unilever.[1]

The rationale for this work was straightforward. Those 15 companies influence the lives of nearly every person in the developed and emerging market world. Collectively, they have the power to change global consumer behaviour and shape a more sustainable future. What better way to reach those consumers than through Facebook?

Just 46 out of 165 consumer brands actively talked about sustainability issues to their Facebook fans during the first six months of 2016. That's only 28 percent of the total brands under study. So what's going wrong? Obviously the problem isn't with the brands' faith in Facebook. It delivers the 165 brands a combined audience of more than 935 million fans – exactly the sort of consumer reach the marketing and advertising community covets.

Neither can it be that brands question consumers' interest in sustainability issues. At least they shouldn't, given the wealth of studies now available showing that consumers (particularly those aged 35 and younger) increasingly make buying decisions based on the transparency and ethical standing of brands, and reject brands they feel don't have their best interests in mind.[2] If marketers needed further convincing of consumer sentiment they should spend some time reading the comments that fans post on the brand Facebook pages.

Forty-three percent of the Facebook pages studied had very active and very vocal comment streams questioning the brand's sustainability commitments, often in the form of concerns over harmful ingredients, working conditions for employees and suppliers, and environmental destruction or pollution.

The problem it would appear is that many brands simply haven't worked out the right tone and approach to talk about social and environmental issues on a social network where they assume Facebookers only want to receive upbeat, jokey encouragement to buy their products.

It's no great surprise that the area where brands feel most comfortable taking ownership of is soft sustainability topics like health and wellness, food and charity work.

Some brands buck the trend. Always, Dove and Aveeno have made issues like self-esteem a core element of their brand marketing and they convey this via Facebook. Sustainable sourcing – not exactly a cuddly type of topic for Facebook brand pages – was also communicated by some Mars Inc. and Unilever brands, specifically sustainable tea, coffee and cocoa initiatives. Most of the alcoholic drink brands offered lip service to responsible drinking (though it was more of a "hygiene" approach than an authentic attempt at reshaping drinking attitudes). More political issues like climate change and clean energy were tougher topics for brands, but not so lesbian, gay, bisexual and transgender (LGBT) issues. In 2016 mainstream US brands were very proactive in taking a stand for equal gender rights.

Instagram

Since 2012 Instagram has been part of the Facebook empire even though its mainly Millennial audience often stays clear of the parent brand.

With its focus on photo and video storytelling (accompanied by deep caption comments and a hashtag-driven taxonomy) Instagram demands a different storytelling discipline than simply relying on reposting blog entries on Facebook and links to them on Twitter.

Not many brands use Instagram for sustainability communication and those that do – mainly lifestyle and clean energy companies – tend to restrict themselves to posting images of sustainability technology or natural beauty that fit with their corporate/brand image.[3]

A few brands have pushed further though. Starbucks used Instagram to promote its KeepCup $1 reusable cup initiative,[4] encouraging people to upload photos of their cups and themselves using those cups to the social network. Nature's Path Organic promotes its non-GMO products and thinking on Instagram,[5] and footwear brand, TOMs, mixes fashion and sustainable lifestyle statements through a portfolio of sunny settings.

Few brands, though, have created a sustainability narrative in quite the way that French NGO Addict Aide did in 2016. It created a fictitious character called Louise Delage (a move that, admittedly, had backfired for brands like L'Oreal in the past),[6] gave her an Instagram account inhabited by a model/actress and, over the course of a few months, started documenting her charmed, free-spirited lifestyle.

The young, attractive social media star attracted over 50,000 likes in a couple of months with bikini-clad photos, snaps of glamorous parties and many stylish dinners. Few of Louise's followers noticed that she was almost always holding an alcoholic drink.

Finally Louise's secret was revealed online. She was actually the star in a public service campaign called Like My Addiction.[7]

Pinterest

For a short time after its launch in 2013, Pinterest was touted to achieve great things in the eyeball-obsessed world of advertising driven social networks.

It didn't quite achieve the world domination of Facebook or even Instagram, but it still commands 175 active users each month[8] and offers a strong brand presence for many retail and fashion brands – mainly because of its 30–50 age female demographic.

A few companies have experimented with Pinterest for sustainability story-telling. Kleenex created a site to offer tips on staying cold- and flu-free. It pins get-well recipe ideas, and tips on avoiding colds and flu, as well as how to tell the difference between the two.[9]

Novartis, meanwhile, used Pinterest to raise awareness for its Malaria Initiative – one of the largest access-to-medicine programs in the health care industry. Working with a range of organisations, the company has provided more than 700 million treatments for adults and children, without profit, to more than 60 malaria-endemic countries, contributing to a significant reduction of the death toll from malaria, mostly infants and children.

To highlight this work and raise awareness about malaria for a younger generation, Novartis created a trading card campaign called M-Force and posted the images of the cards on Pinterest. Each card portrays a superhero with powers to fight Plasmorpheus, the Malaria Mutant.[10] Eli Lily, in a similar vein, pinned many of the entries in its annual Oncology on Canvas art competition.[11]

Snapchat

Every day, more than 100 million people – the vast majority under the age of 30 – use Snapchat, the smartphone-only social network that launched in 2011.[12] While consumer brands continue to experiment with marketing that works for the platform – in 2017 Audi teamed up with The Onion in a high-profile Superbowl campaign[13] – Snapchat has proved harder for sustainability marketers to master, with some exceptions.

Everlane, the five-year-old online clothing brand with a strong commitment to transparency, offers frequent updates of what's going on behind the scenes at Everlane headquarters and hosts Transparency Tuesdays, where the social media team answers users' questions about the company,[14] as well as offering tours of their factory for fans and customers.[15]

In 2015 AOL turned to Snapchat as part of a drive to recruit more Millennial-age women to work at the company. AOL ran two 10-second Snapchat videos in the app's Discover section – where publishers post daily content – and in the Live Stories part of the app. The first promoted a hashtag #BuiltbyGirls, to raise awareness for BBV Venture, which invests in women-led start-ups. The other spot showed 10-second video shots of people working at AOL, including AOL Build, the brand's live interview series. As a result of the mini-campaign, AOL saw an 18 percent increase in female Millennial applicants.[16]

GE has been one of the most inventive users of Snapchat (as it has proved on so many other social media platforms). In 2014 it took over an NYU Chemistry lab as part of its #EmojiScience to show how science can be engaging and relatable to younger students and sent videos of live science experiments to its

Snapchat followers. The company also encouraged fans to send their favourite emojis to GE's Snapchat handle. It then replied with a video experiment that evoked each specific emoji.[17]

When it comes to understanding Snapchat's real potential, however, no brand has done a better job than Unilever's Dove. In 2014, as part of the brand's long-running commitment to raising female self-esteem, it hosted a Snapchat safe chat space where women could talk with a small team of psychologists and other brand ambassadors to share ideas and concerns about self-esteem issues. At the end of the each chat, the conversation disappeared – as all Snapchats do. It was a small-scale endeavour – the two-hour chat attracted 75 individual conversations and 130,000 views – but it offered a fascinating best-practice example of understanding both the power of social media and the strengths of Snapchat in particular.

Tumblr

One of GE's most interesting social media publishing platforms sits on Tumblr, the hybrid blog/social network now owned by Yahoo.

The GE Tumblr contains posts exploring the changing worlds of science and tech – from archive photos and film clips covering GE's long history, to up-to-date content on sustainable tech and the importance of STEM to produce ideas for the future.

Tumblr, with its focus on fashion and food, might seem an odd platform for a brand as industrial as GE. Yet, by creating custom content, rather than simply repurposing posts to Facebook or the corporate magazines, GE has created something fresh that resonates with Tumblr's geeky technologist community.

IBM is another company that has succeeded on Tumblr by playing to the geeks. Over the years it has created a number of different Tumblr accounts including ones devoted to Smarter Cities and Smarter Planet, as well as its innovation-focused IBMblr.

Twitter

This is one of life's great mysteries: how can Twitter be so important to world events and yet so frustrating to be part of?

Few things in life evoke such a love/hate reaction as Twitter. In fact, you might say that there are only two types of people in life: those who love Twitter and those who have burned out on Twitter. It is the social channel most used by sustainability communicators – and yet what real value do they get from it?

There's no denying Twitter's power. Presidents use it to trump the media and set global agendas, after all. But when it comes to sustainability communications Twitter feels at best like little more than a glorified newswire.

At worst it resembles a spam cannon for the public relations industry – a platform, to paraphrase Shakespeare, full of sound and fury but signifying nothing.

Part of the reason why so many people feel exhausted by Twitter is the pure volume of noise and tweets that flow through Twitter every few minutes. The same attributes that make the network a must-visit at times of crisis and breaking news contribute to the sense of information overload on issues where you crave depth and clarity. As Twitter has become ubiquitous for communicators so it has lost a great deal of its relevance.

Some will argue that Twitter remains an energetic forum for debate about sustainability issues. That may well be true but, if that is the case, it is a debate taking place among a niche audience of like-minded souls. There's no harm in that because at least communicators know they can reach a targeted audience of peers, NGOs, media and other interested stakeholders using Twitter. The danger is that by continually preaching to the choir, Twitter becomes little more than an echo chamber for the corporate sustainability community rather than a platform to engage and inspire sustainability action on a bigger scale.

YouTube

YouTube could be a perfect medium for communicating sustainability but, for the most part, the Google-owned video network is a wasteland when it comes to sustainability storytelling – a dumping ground of bad corporate talking heads or dull but worthy low-fi documentary footage of far-flung corporate social responsibility campaigns.

In both cases, the content that companies want to highlight is important and could find an audience if only it was conceived and executed better. But most companies waste their YouTube moment. Just consider the stats: in 2015 Sustainly researched 85 sustainability themed videos made by 25 companies (chosen from a mix of industry sectors). In total those 85 videos were viewed 37.5 million times. Yet just eight of those videos had more than 1 million views and just 20 in total could claim more than 100,000 views. Twenty-four videos from these big corporates had been viewed less than 1,000 times.[18]

Of course there are some obvious exceptions to this video mediocrity. Shakira's 2014 World Cup collaboration with Danone brand Activia in aid of the World Food Programme was viewed 400 million times. And YouTube is one of the channels where companies promote their documentary work.

Don't put your eggs all in one basket

At the time of this writing, the social networks profiled were still going strong. Yet such is the fast-changing social media landscape there is no guarantee that all or any of these current mainstream media giant killers will still be around in five years.

Since the first blogging platform, LiveJournal, launched back in 1999, more than a dozen social platforms, apps and networks have either shut down, gone dormant or been often subsumed into larger networks.

Ultimately, from a communication point of view, the key for brands is to have an editorial mentality rather than a platform mentality. Platforms come and go, and those that remain often change their terms and conditions as Twitter and Facebook have shown or realign their business models as Medium did in early 2017.

Notes

1 https://sustainly.com/news/2016/12/06/big-brand-report-2016
2 www.credit-suisse.com/microsites/next/en/entrepreneurism/articles/millennials-drive-sustainability.html
3 http://adage.com/article/digital/instagram-stories-appeal-snapchat-brands/305317/
4 www.keepcup.com/
5 www.instagram.com/naturespathorganic/
6 Back in 2005, in one of the first major social media faux pas, L'Oreal created a fake blog in the voice of a young, pretty woman who wrote about her skincare experiences – all favourable for L'Oreal of course. It was quickly exposed as a marketing stunt.
7 www.adweek.com/adfreak/who-louise-delage-troubling-truth-behind-overnight-instagram-success-173792
8 www.adweek.com/digital/pinterest-175-million-monthly-active-users/
9 www.pinterest.com/Kleenex/cold-flu-free/
10 www.pinterest.com/novartis/m-force-trading-cards/
11 www.pinterest.com/llyonconcanvas/
12 www.inc.com/sujan-patel/10-brands-you-should-follow-on-snapchat-immediately.html
13 www.hugeinc.com/case-study/super-bowl-snapchat
14 http://fashionista.com/2016/05/snapchat-fashion-brands
15 http://tumblr.everlane.com/post/101946096903/were-here-to-make-a-bold-claim-snapchat-is-going
16 www.adweek.com/digital/how-aol-used-snapchat-recruitment-tool-millennial-women-171803/
17 http://digiday.com/marketing/latest-ge-pop-emoji-science-lab/
18 The 5th Annual Social Media Sustainability Index, page 20

Chapter 11

How to save the sustainability report

How much does your company spend on its glossy sustainability or corporate social responsibility report each year? Does it really help you connect with your community or is it merely nice sustainability window dressing? Have you ever wondered why exactly companies bother producing sustainability reports at all?

That's not to belittle sustainability reporting. Non-financial reporting is a crucial part of embedding sustainability within the organisation and should play a key role demonstrating authenticity to outside stakeholders – hence rebuilding trust.

But while sustainability reporting is crucial to the integrity and future direction of every company, producing a bloated, overly designed and overly expensive sustainability report definitely is not.

The time has come to reposition sustainability reporting at the heart of corporate decision-making so that it can inform, connect and mobilise all areas of the business – but especially finance, operations and marketing – around sustainable business strategy.

Most Fortune 500 and FTSE 100 companies have been reporting on non-financial issues for at least the last 10 years. Over that period the report, and the type of issues disclosed, has changed dramatically as companies have shifted their focus from corporate social responsibility to sustainability issues that are core to business performance. And yet very few companies integrate both their financial and non-financial (sustainability) reporting into one document – so helping sustainability resonate and make sense for shareholders. Even fewer integrate sustainability metrics into their financial reporting. As a result the voluntary reporting standards that most companies now comply with – such as the Global Reporting Initiative and the Carbon Disclosure Project – often fail to penetrate the core financial planning and accounting that dictates the future direction the business will take.

At the moment, then, many companies are making short- and long-term financial assessments without having access to a complete set of data about the risks and opportunities that lie ahead. As issues like climate change, resource scarcity, transparent supply chains and equality within the workforce have an ever bigger impact on companies' bottom line, so sustainability reporting will need to grow in importance for companies, and be married to traditional financial reporting and planning, as they seek to show that they are running successful and responsible operations.

A number of sustainable finance initiatives are pursuing this purpose. The Natural Capital Coalition, for example, helps companies assess their direct and indirect interactions with the world's stock of natural capital (including geology, soil, air, water and all biodiversity). It has developed the Natural Capital and Social Capital Protocols to help companies effectively measure and report their environmental and social costs. Reporting 3.0, meanwhile, is a non-profit organisation that brings together companies, consultants and NGOs to help "create a global multi-stakeholder community focused on identifying and fulfilling the potential of reporting to serve the intersecting interests of sustainability, financial performance, and growth."[1]

Regulation is also nudging companies in the right direction. New European Union laws require most mid-sized and large companies to report on non-financial issues including environmental issues, social and employee aspects of the business, respect for human rights, anti-corruption and bribery issues, and diversity in their boards of directors.

A smarter way of communicating sustainability reporting

The pressure on companies to produce more accurate and financially relevant sustainability reporting will come from many stakeholders, including employees, shareholders, the media and the general public, and it will propelled by new commitments that companies have pledged to meet – the United Nations Sustainable Development Goals being particularly prominent (as is discussed in Chapter 12).

In this environment where understanding and acting on sustainability pressures will be key for business performance, legal compliance and corporate reputation, the importance of communicating sustainability reporting cannot be overstated.

For the last decade most sustainability reports have been published as a glossy print publication and distributed online as a PDF download or sometimes as an interactive microsite. These niche publications cost hundreds of thousands of pounds to produce, only to languish under the desks of the stakeholders who receive them or be balkanised in the farthest recesses of a company's website. Simply put, the sustainability report in its current form is not doing justice to the time, effort and money being put into it.

Admittedly, sustainability reports tend to be focused on a very small niche of very important stakeholders. The general public has never been the target audience. But that doesn't mean the information being collected and reported isn't of interest and value to a wider audience.

Now that the public is demanding more information about sustainability, corporate communicators and marketers have to be more creative, useful and transparent in the way they impart sustainability information. Producing smarter sustainability reports is a good place to start.

For too many companies the sustainability report is the pinnacle of their sustainability communications each year when it should be just the starting point – the launch pad even – for a sustainability conversation with the investors, NGOs, the media, employees and, yes, the public.

This is an opportunity lost because the information that sits within all sustainability reports is a potential goldmine for interacting with real people and demonstrating to them what many still have a hard time believing: namely that companies are making concrete efforts to make their operations sustainable and to make products and services that put the needs of the consumers first.

Rather than looking at the sustainability report as the dull but worthy end result of a lengthy research process, companies should consider their reports as the raw materials for great storytelling. Take those environmental, social and governance data and repackage them to meet the interests and needs of non-sustainability experts. Evaluate all the feedback about the company's social commitments and create real human stories. Overall, analyse the hard data and anecdotal evidence that have been compiled and use them in more creative, engaging ways to demonstrate the company's commitment and authenticity.

A word of warning, though: there's no point in having a wonderfully creative sustainability report if the storytelling isn't backed up by the facts. Just ask Volkswagen, whose 2014 sustainability report – published just as the company was being exposed for its massive diesel emissions fraud – was described by HuffPost as a "horrible joke".[2]

Eight ways companies made their sustainability reports more relevant to the public

Companies love big reports and white papers. There's something about producing volumes of paper or digital pages that conveys gravitas or "thought leadership" in the minds of corporate communicators. This is particularly true with sustainability reports – an annual or bi-annual opportunity to cram all a company's responsible thinking and work into one big publication.

While there's nothing wrong with having a comprehensive sustainability report, too many companies fail to appreciate just how the information in the report could be packaged and shared online to inform and gain the respect of a wider audience.

Here then are eight examples of recent sustainability reports that were designed to appeal beyond the traditional stakeholder readership.

Example 1. Real voices are better than corporate speak

How to reinvent the boring old sustainability report? If you're Heineken you commission a spoken word version. The Netherlands-based beverage giant turned to spoken-word artist Kevin "Blaxtar" de Randamie to reinterpret the information in its 2015 sustainability report.

This could have gone spectacularly wrong. Just ask Samsung: the tech company also commissioned a rap version of its sustainability report, but the end result drew incredulity from the social media world back in 2014 and promptly disappeared from Samsung's corporate site.[3]

Heineken's spoken word interpretation, titled *Let's Get Frank,* is more sophisticated, lyrical and, yes, cerebral. In the video performance Blaxtar rhymes on themes like sustainable sourcing, the role of African farmers in local agriculture, reduced CO_2 emissions, and water scarcity in a style that both informs and grabs the audience's attention. This, of course, is the whole point of the experiment – to engage a new audience around the sustainability work Heineken is undertaking through a medium more accessible than the PDF.

In some ways Blaxtar's performance is just an extension of the many apps, animations and infographics that companies have employed to breathe life into sustainability reports in recent years. Yet there's also no denying that a spoken-word version of a report also breaks new ground – taking a chance, in this instance, that Heineken drinkers want to know about core sustainability issues that they may not necessarily search out for themselves.

Example 2. Recruit an influencer

Heineken took its sustainability social media outreach in a different direction by working with YouTuber and Instagrammer Ben Brown to document its Brewed by the Sun environmental strategy.

Brown is a filmmaker and photographer whose stock in trade is creating travel-experience videos (and drinking quite a lot of beer) to share with his 600,000 YouTube subscribers, most of whom are young males between 25 and 35 years old – just the demographic Heineken wants to talk to. The company sent him to Singapore to discover and document how Tiger beer is being brewed using solar power as well as to Austria to see how the Gosser brewery is 100 percent carbon free.

Example 3. Animate with relevance

As part of its 2013 integrated annual report, global paint and chemical manufacturer AkzoNobel created a series of animated video case studies to highlight its environmental performance.[4]

Four different videos showed the priorities areas for AkzoNobel, including *Doing More with Less* and *Making Roads Safer*. Each video demonstrated AkzoNobel's commitment to make the chemical industry safer, less toxic and more transparent with the help of easy-to-grasp animation and a jaunty voice-over. It might be a stretch to say that these videos made coatings and biochemical really interesting for the general public, but they succeeded in communicating a very complicated topic in a more digestible way.

Example 4. Keep sustainability on brand

To make its sustainability report more accessible, Apple created a sleek and slick environment section within its website to house performance data and targets for reducing its impact on the environment.

Famously acclaimed as one of the best design companies in the world, there is the expectation that all things that come from Apple HQ will be beautifully designed with the user experience in the forefront. Its sustainability section supports this. Using motion graphics and trademark Apple visuals, the company shares its efforts of reducing waste, water and energy in its operations and outlines its future ambitions.

As with all things Apple, the sustainability section and report is minimalist and engaging – and on brand.

Example 5. Connect sustainability to products

Few brands tell sustainability stories through their actual products. Levi Strauss bucked that trend in 2014 when it dedicated part of its sustainability report to the lifecycle of jeans using interactive diagrams and infographics to show the environmental impact of each one of its products.[5] This includes criteria like land occupation, water used in production, renewable energy and land transportation.

Aside from making the technical information easy to understand, Levi Strauss created benchmarks so that consumers can evaluate the type of jean they can see has a lower environmental impact, potentially helping them make more sustainable choices.

Example 6. Visualise the journey

Consistently regarded as a leader in environmental practices and often ranked among the top three of most sustainable companies in the world, Natura, Brazil's largest cosmetics company, turned its sustainability report into an illustrated slide journey complete with Facebook comments built in.[6]

A section dedicated to social biodiversity showed information about Natura's commitment to the Amazon by taking the viewer inside its production processes and supplying relevant investment facts. An animated slide journey introduced features such as Natura's "Ecoparque" – a facility to foster community development in the Amazon.

Example 7. Sustainability in 100 facts

To celebrate a century in business, German car maker BMW created a sustainability fact book titled *100 Years, 100 Facts.*[7]

Available as a downloadable PDF from the main sustainability site, the fact book was an automotive geek's dream guide to sustainable mobility, highlighting the company's electric vehicle development and its innovation in hydrogen-powered vehicles, plus new design elements for its petrol and diesel cars that reduce emissions and increase safety.

Example 8. Reports come alive

In 2012 Kering set a series of sustainability targets to achieve by 2016, focusing on environmental and social challenges ranging from leather traceability and responsible gold sourcing to water pollution, chemical use and carbon emissions.

In 2016 it reported back on its achievements and accompanied the publication of its report with a live webinar hosted by a broadcast journalist and featuring Kering's head of sustainability, Marie-Claire Daveu.[8]

During the 35-minute webinar attendees could submit questions in real time via Facebook and Twitter and Daveu responded to each one.

Q&A with Michael Dickstein, former director of global sustainable development for Heineken (until June 2017)

Q: Why does sustainability matter to Heineken as a business?

A: When we started out with our sustainability agenda about 15 years ago, the rationale was more of an altruistic nature. We have traditionally a large presence in Africa so we engaged in HIV protection for our employees and their families. More and more we saw the alcohol agenda emerging and, in order to retain commercial freedom, we wanted to demonstrate that we are a responsible business. During the next phase, we engaged in more sustainability topics that make business sense. Think of our water and raw materials agenda – they relate closely to risk mitigation. For example, we have identified 23 breweries around the world that operate in water scarce areas either now or potentially in the future. So focusing on them and making sure the water catchment areas will be sustainable over time is not just a corporate social responsibility topic; it means addressing a key operational risk which perfectly supports our long-term business.

The more work we did, the more we discovered sustainable business opportunities. Our Brewed by the Sun programme links our brands to renewable energy – the production of beers like Gösser, Moretti and Tiger are powered by solar panels at the breweries. We have now more than 50,000 of those panels installed worldwide. Ultimately I firmly believe that a sustainability strategy that is not embedded in the business strategy will not be sustainable in itself.

Q: How important is it to communicate sustainability to all your stakeholders?

A: What sense would it make to do the best things in the world if you are not talking about them? We are committed to be an open and transparent business and to engage proactively with our stakeholders. What is key, though, is that we are not just sharing our success stories. Look for instance at our 2015 sustainability report – we were equally open about the areas where we hadn't made the progress we then wanted to.

Q: Sustainability topics like responsible drinking are no longer seen just as niche topics to be communicated. What changed?

A: The whole moderation campaign, as we call it, is now fully owned by marketing; they are driving the agenda. That wasn't the case 10 to 15 years ago. I still remember a time when doors were rather closed as they basically said, "You CSR guys are either limiting our creativity or you are telling us to fill in questionnaires and surveys without knowing the value of this exercise to the business."

However, in recent years topics like responsible consumption are actually well received by consumers, if communicated in an engaging manner. The brand equity of the Heineken brand has significantly increased thanks to campaigns such as Dance More, Drink Slow. Our marketeers love this story and they fully embrace it.

That said, you have to approach sustainability marketing in a credible way. Marketing for the Heineken brand is usually aiming at the little twinkle in your eye. Sustainability brand public relations needs to adopt that tone intrinsically or you won't catch that certain authenticity in your brand appearance.

Q: Heineken has also targeted resource scarcity and climate change through sustainability communication – notably the *Let's Get Frank* spoken-word video and online games associated with your sustainability reports. Was this considered a success?

A: Yes, absolutely. But you have to be very careful with related stakeholder segmentation. What works for one target audience won't necessarily work for another. Take the case of Ben Brown, the vlogger who we asked to tour our Tiger solar-powered brewery in Singapore as well as the world's first large-scale green brewery in Göss/Austria. I'll be honest in admitting that I didn't even know what a vlogger was before the idea was proposed – and I was probably not the only one in my age category. Yet Ben's videos about our sustainability work have now been watched by millions of people – far more than we could have reached with traditional stakeholder communication. The same is true with *Let's Get Frank*. We didn't focus with this video on our traditional report audience, who read it for the data and numbers. However, the spoken-word video helped us reach a different and far bigger audience who normally wouldn't engage with a sustainability report.

Notes

1 http://reporting3.org/
2 www.huffingtonpost.com/entry/volkswagen-sustainability-report-from-last-year-is-a-joke_us_56040f1ae4b0fde8b0d17996
3 http://sustainly.com/content/article/362/samsung-gets-bad-rap-its-sustainability-report-video
4 http://report.akzonobel.com/2013/ar/case-studies/doing-more-with-less.html
5 http://levistrauss.com/wp-content/uploads/2015/03/Full-LCA-Results-Deck-FINAL.pdf
6 www.relatoweb.com.br/natura/13/en/social-biodiversity
7 www.bmwgroup.com/content/dam/bmw-group-websites/bmwgroup_com/responsibility/downloads/en/2016/e_100100_Factbook_2016.pdf
8 https://live-secure.brainsonic.com/kering/20160503/standard/global.php

Chapter 12

Global Goals for winning trust

Sustainability is moving rapidly from the corporate backroom into the mainstream. Faced with a future of uncertain energy costs, looming regulation on carbon emissions, concerns about access to raw materials and the availability of natural resources like water, companies all over the world are waking up to the reality that environmental sustainability is a key consideration. At the same time those same companies are coming under greater scrutiny about their role in society – as has been documented throughout this book.

As companies navigate this uncertain business landscape, communicating a cohesive vision of environmental and social sustainability will be crucial to win the trust and respect of customers, employees, shareholders, investors and the media. But how many in the communication and creative sectors really understand the issues that lie at the heart of sustainable business?

The answer is, not that many. So now is the time for the worlds of advertising, marketing, public relations and corporate communication to get sustainability smart. Luckily, what once might have seemed a very arduous and technical education has been made much simpler with the widespread adoption of the United Nations Sustainable Development Goals (SDGs).

Formally adopted at the United Nations general assembly in September 2015, the 17 environmental and social goals provide a blueprint for sustainable growth for the business world. They make a priority issues such as eradicating poverty, providing everyone with equal opportunities for economic growth, erasing gender inequality and tackling climate change to name just four. The goals took two years to negotiate and have global governmental backing – 193 nations agreed to adopt them. They are not legally binding but look set to influence international, national and regional regulations. For companies the goals will likely act as a de facto license to operate in many parts of the world.

The goals could also prove to be the most important bridge between the worlds of finance, sustainability and marketing/communications – not least because of their potential to fully integrate sustainability, business operations and financial reporting within companies.

Most business leaders already understand that sustainability concerns have a profound influence on their companies' performance. The problem is that, up until now, they have lacked an effective framework to translate sustainability and other non-financial information into future financial performance.

In the past, these issues may have seemed removed from the calculations of everyday business partly because of the disconnect between financial and non-financial reporting (as explored in Chapter 11). The SDGs offer a great opportunity to bridge that gap and create a fully rounded way of assessing a business – one that values a company's role in the ecosystem where it operates and benchmarks it against the objectives being set by global society.

By helping the financial heart of the business understand the risks and opportunities associated with sustainability issues, the SDGs will speed up the adoption and integration of sustainability into mainstream strategy and action. When sustainability stops being considered a side issue you can also be sure that it will become a priority for marketing and communications – as it already is in a growing number of leading companies.

Ultimately the SDGs could yet become the lingua franca for all of business to understand, plan, execute and communicate sustainable business. Before that can happen, though, companies and employees will need a better understanding of the Global Goals and how they will impact their business and careers.

The Global Goals guide for business

Which of the Global Goals are most important for different companies? The simple answer is that all 17 should be a priority for all companies but, in reality, companies will focus on the ones they believe are most material for their operations and sustainable footprint.

The financial services sector will no doubt see Goal 8 (Decent Work and Economic Growth) and Goal 10 (Reduced Inequalities) as key areas where it can deliver expertise. Financial services also has an overarching role in mobilising the finance needed (an estimated $3 to $4 trillion per year in public and private funds[1]) for the goals to succeed.

The health care industry has obvious responsibilities in supporting Goal 3 (Good Health and Well-Being) and the food industry must play a supersized role in Goal 2 (Zero Hunger), while the technology and industrial sectors have leadership roles to play in meeting Goals 9 (Industry, Innovation and Infrastructure) and 11 (Sustainable Cities and Communities).

Other goals, however, will require companies to have a more holistic and expansive vision of sustainability. Goal 14 (Life Below Water) for example isn't just about the maritime and fishing industries. Every business that uses plastic packaging has a major impact on life under water given the millions of tonnes of plastic that are polluting our oceans: up to 80 percent of the plastic in the ocean is from land-based sources.[2] It is a similar story with Goal 15 (Life on Land).

Here, then, is a look at the 17 goals and some thoughts about the ways companies can be most effective in making them a success.

Goal 1. No Poverty

Goal 1 aims to end to all poverty by 2030 and ensure social protection for the poor and vulnerable wherever they are in the world. It would guarantee access to basic services and support people harmed by climate-related extreme events and other economic, social, and environmental shocks and disasters. The top target is to eradicate extreme poverty for all people everywhere, which is currently measured as people living on less than $1.25 a day.

The United Nations particularly wants to see the expansion of social protection programmes such as cash transfers, school feeding and targeted food assistance, as well as social insurance and labour market programmes, including old-age pensions, disability pensions, unemployment insurance and skills training, and wage subsidies, among others.

How companies can help meet the goal

The entire financial services sector has a leading role to play in meeting this goal. For example, Visa, in conjunction with other financial services providers, aims to provide access to financial services for 500 million unbanked people. MasterCard, for its part, with $11 million of funding from its charitable foundation, has established an innovation lab in East Africa aiming to expand digital financial services to 100 million people globally.[3] Other companies with a global supply chain and operations in developing nations also have a role to play.

Goal 2. Zero Hunger

The aim of Goal 2 is to end hunger and all forms of malnutrition by 2030. It also seeks to ensure universal access to safe, nutritious and sufficient food. Some 795 million people (that's one in nine on earth) don't get enough food to lead a healthy, active life and three-quarters of all undernourished people in the world live in rural areas.[4]

A central target is to ensure access by all people – in particular the poor and people in vulnerable situations, including infants – to safe, nutritious and sufficient food all year round. A secondary target is to end all forms of malnutrition and address the nutritional needs of adolescent girls, pregnant and lactating women and older persons.

This will require sustainable food production systems and resilient agricultural practices; and equal access to land, technology and markets; as well as international cooperation on investments in infrastructure and technology to boost agricultural productivity.

How companies can meet the goal

Naturally, food producers are taking a strong leadership role in tackling hunger and malnutrition issues around the world.

In Nigeria, Unilever brand Knorr has pioneered a new type of vegetable bouillon cube with added iron to help combat chronic iron deficiency among women and young children. Nestlé has a similar programme in India, while Cargill's Nourishing India platform has reached 25 million customers with its edible oil brands, fortified with essential vitamins A, D and E.[5]

Other industries are also playing a role. Philips City Farming Program works with universities and partners to develop indoor commercial farms using LED grow lights. Farming by this method can result in 20–25 harvests a year, with up to 85 percent less energy usage. Eli Lilly's animal health division, Elanco, has been developing technologies that protect animals from infectious disease, reduce the environmental impact of livestock production, enhance animal well-being and eradicate food-borne illness. These enable farmers and producers to provide greater amounts of food safely and sustainably.[6]

Goal 3. Good Health and Well-Being

Goal 3 aims to guarantee health and well-being for all. It encompasses reproductive, maternal and child health; access to safe, effective, quality and affordable medicines and vaccines; and targets communicable, non-communicable and environmental diseases.

Key targets for this SDG include reducing the number of mothers who die in childbirth, preventing unintended pregnancies through better sexual and reproductive health education, and continuing the fight against major infectious diseases including HIV, tuberculosis and malaria. Tackling environmental conditions and road traffic accidents (especially in fast-expanding urban locations) and reducing mental health problems and substance abuse (including tobacco and alcohol) also are identified as key targets for meeting global health goals.

How companies can help meet the goal

Many multinational brands are active in improving health. They include obvious candidates from the pharmaceutical sector including Novo Nordisk (malaria) and Novartis AG, which launched Novartis Access in 2015, a portfolio of 15 medicines to treat chronic diseases in low- and lower-middle income countries.[7] Consumer goods giants, meanwhile, like Unilever,

Kimberly-Clark, RB and P&G, all have vested interests in improving education around issues like self-esteem and sexual health. Increasingly, health care providers are looking to encourage proactive health action in the form of wellness projects.

Diageo and Heineken continue to invest in drinking education programs while AB InBev launched a series of Global Smart Drinking Goals – the first of which aims to reduce the harmful use of alcohol by at least 10 percent in all of their markets by the end of 2025, by working with governments, civil society and public health experts to change social norms and behaviours.[8]

From a technology point of view, GE is manufacturing low-cost medical equipment to address medical equipment shortages in emerging markets. The company has opened a number of manufacturing facilities in India, with an extended line of products including ultrasound machines, ECG units, and maternal and infant care equipment. Siemens AG runs Mobile Clinics which bring health care to underserved communities in India.

Goal 4. Quality Education

The aim of Goal 4 is to guarantee a quality education for all, particularly through basic cognitive and language skills, and fostering emotional development. At present some 59 million children of primary-school age have no formal education, and many of those who do are failing to get a satisfactory grounding in core skills such as reading and mathematics.[9]

Goal 4 strongly supports education for girls and for the poor. A central target includes ensuring all girls and boys have access to quality early childhood development, care and pre-primary education so that they are ready for primary education. The goal also looks to substantially increase the number of youth and adults who have relevant technical and vocational skills for employment.

How companies can help meet the goal

Companies invest heavily in promoting education around the world partly because it is an issue where they can demonstrate real leadership with little risk of criticism, but also because they understand the importance of developing diverse talent in a global marketplace. Technology, industrial services and media companies including Pearson, Microsoft, Verizon and Google have led the push to promote STEM education programmes and campaigns – especially for young female school and college students. LEGO has developed STEM Programs to create environments where learning happens in a hands-on and motivational way, helping young students discover their talents and cement learning using solutions such as LEGO's Simple Machines and WeDo.

Goal 5. Gender Equality

The aim of Goal 5 is to promote gender equality globally. The overarching target is to end all forms of discrimination against all women and girls everywhere. It also calls for the elimination of all forms of violence against all women and girls, including trafficking and sexual and other types of exploitation. Stopping harmful practices – such as early and forced marriage, and female genital mutilation – is another priority, as is recognising and valuing unpaid care and domestic work through the provision of public services, infrastructure and social protection policies.

The goal seeks to ensure universal access to sexual and reproductive health and reproductive rights, and to enhance the use of technology, in particular information and communications technology, to promote the empowerment of women.

How companies can help meet the goal

In the developing world, some of the biggest multinationals are looking to support gender equality through support and enablement programmes.

Nestlé's Action Plan on Women in the Cocoa Supply Chain, which operates in Cote d'Ivoire, works to create equal opportunities by giving women a voice and improving their income. In Costa Rica Illy invested in a female-run coffee collective (as documented in Chapter 9).

Other companies have made gender equality in the workplace a priority, including PwC with its Women in Work index and its aim to achieve gender parity in its own workforce.

Goal 6. Clean Water and Sanitation

Goal 6 states, "water and sanitation are at the very core of sustainable development, critical to the survival of people and the planet." The goal relates to drinking water, sanitation and hygiene, as well as the quality and sustainability of water resources worldwide.

The overarching target is to achieve universal and equitable access to safe and affordable drinking water for all. Another target is achieving access to adequate and equitable sanitation and hygiene for all (including ending open defecation) with special attention given to the needs of women and girls and those in vulnerable situations. The goal also seeks to improve water quality by reducing pollution, eliminating dumping and minimising the release of hazardous chemicals and materials – so halving the proportion of untreated wastewater and substantially increasing recycling and safe water reuse.

How companies can help meet the goal

The sustainable supply of freshwater sources will only grow as an issue of concern over the coming years. Both global business and society will be in competition for depleted supplies and the ways that companies manage their water resources will have major impacts on their corporate reputations, profitability and their standing in society.

Clorox, Kimberly-Clark, Johnson & Johnson, P&G and Unilever all have made strong sustainable product and campaign commitments to tackling sanitation issues. The latter, for example, developed a new soap that offers better protection against bacteria that cause stomach infections, typhoid and cholera, and that also combats skin and eye infections[10]. Other companies like Levi Strauss and Coca-Cola are taking concrete steps to reduce the amount of water they use in their operations. But all companies still have an enormous water usage footprint – an Achilles heel that will pose problems for them in the near future.

Goal 7. Affordable and Clean Energy

The aim of Goal 7 is to enable the supply of affordable and clean energy worldwide. It is also a crucial pillar in achieving many of the other SDGs.

More than a billion people worldwide still don't have access to electricity, though the global flight to the cities is reducing this disparity. Eighty percent of people who have gotten access to electricity since 2010 are urban dwellers.

Even as the world embraces renewable fuels, it is also getting more efficient with the energy that is created. Globally, energy intensity (the amount of energy it takes to fuel economic output) decreased by 1.7 percent per year from 2010 to 2012. Some 68 percent of the savings in energy intensity has come from developing regions, with Eastern Asia as the largest contributor.[11]

How companies can help meet the goal

Reducing energy use and moving away from fossil fuel dependency have been central sustainability goals of most major companies. However, major utilities and energy companies have particular responsibilities. Solar and wind providers such as Iberdrola, Vestas and Acciona already lead in this area. Others, such as Denmark's Orsted, are transforming their operations to move away from fossil fuels.

Industrial services and technology companies are equally keen to play a part.

Caterpillar entered a strategic alliance in 2015 with First Solar to provide solar power to remote villages where, before now, electric power has been either unavailable or unreliable. And Tesla is pushing ahead with plans to provide large-format home batteries to store power generated by solar energy.[12]

Goal 8. Decent Work and Economic Growth

The aim of Goal 8 – ensuring sustained and inclusive economic growth – is another pillar for achieving sustainable development, even if it might seem an obvious area of concern for sustainability professionals. It sets a 2030 target of full and productive employment and decent work for all women and men, including young people and persons with disabilities, and equal pay for work of equal value.

A central target is to end forced labour, slavery and human trafficking as well as stop child labour in all its forms. This goal also looks to bolster domestic financial institutions to expand access to banking, insurance and financial services for all – with a particular focus on helping women as financial exclusion disproportionately affects women and the poor. Sustainable tourism is seen as one way to deliver decent work opportunities for the poor in the developing world.

How companies can help meet the goal

Access to financial services plays an important role in realising this goal. Companies like Credit Suisse run regional microfinance funds that provide working capital to agricultural cooperatives so they can support low-income farmers. Other firms look to work collectively. Citi and Visa Inc. have collaborated with the Bill & Melinda Gates Foundation, The Ford Foundation, Omidyar Network and USAID to build the Better Than Cash Alliance. It helps people in emerging economies transition to e-payment systems.

In the tech sector, Hewlett-Packard (HP) has worked to eradicate exploitative labour practices and forced labour throughout its supply chain. It was the first tech company to require direct employment of foreign migrant workers in its supply chain through the HP Supply Chain Foreign Migrant Worker Standard.

Goal 9. Industry, Innovation and Infrastructure

The aim of Goal 9 covers three important elements of sustainable development: infrastructure, industrialisation and innovation. It targets upgrading infrastructure and rethinking industries to make them sustainable. It stresses the need for increased resource efficiency and the greater adoption of clean and environmentally sound technologies and industrial processes. Making those improvements will involve increased access to financial services (especially credit) as well as technical and technological support.

The goal aims to increase scientific research, dramatically improve access to information and communications technology, and strive to provide universal and affordable access to the Internet in the least developed countries by 2020. Over the past decade mobile cellular services have spread rapidly around the world. Today 69 percent of the global population lives in areas covered by mobile broadband networks. However, the share of coverage in rural areas is just 29 percent.[13]

How companies can help meet the goal

Many multinational companies are focusing their energy on sustainable infrastructure, including telecom providers like Virgin and tech giants like Google and Cisco. In Mexico basic materials company, Cemex, created the programme Mejora tu Calle to help communities and governments collaborate to improve neighbourhoods using its cement products. Through this programme, the company provides microloans to community members to help fund the pavement of streets and sidewalks with cement. Since inception, more than 35,000 microloans have been allocated to finance paving over 400,000 square meters, benefiting more than 7,000 low-income families.[14]

Goal 10. Reduced Inequalities

SDG 10 aims to reduce inequalities in income as well as empower and promote the social, economic and political inclusion of all, irrespective of age, sex, disability, race, ethnicity, origin, religion or economic or other status. The goal considers inequality both between countries and within individual nations. A central part of this goal is making sure that income growth among the poorest 40 percent of the population in every country rises quicker than the national average. That means guaranteeing fair wages, creating jobs and protecting social policies during a period where increased technological efficiencies and automation are altering the global employment landscape.

Another major factor in reducing inequalities will be fixing the inherent imbalances in the global financial system – notably issues like tax havens and tax evasion policies as well as enabling investment opportunities to fund real sustainable development in societies.

How companies can help meet the goal

Hiring and developing a more inclusive workforce is a key consideration for companies in regard to Goal 10. This has become a major priority for financial and professional service sector giants who hire thousands of graduate employees globally each year. Improving the quality of jobs on offer, and putting career growth training and policies in place will help companies hold onto talent.

Addressing inequalities also becomes important in terms of corporate reputation with consumers. In the United States, companies as varied as PepsiCo, Target and Apple have taken strong stances in support of the LGBT community.

GM has 12 Employee Resource Groups that provide a forum for employees to share common concerns and experiences, gain professional development support and engage in local communities. These groups include the African Ancestry Network, Asian Indian Affinity Group, Chinese Employee Resource

Group, GM Hispanic Initiative Team, Native American Cultural Network, and People With Disabilities. All Employee Resource Groups work towards making GM a workplace of choice and they provide insights that help GM better understand diverse and emerging consumer markets.[15]

Goal 11. Sustainable Cities and Communities

More than half the world's population lives in cities – a figure that will increase dramatically through the rest of this century. Cities then will play a central role in the future of the planet. The aim of Goal 11 is to make them centres of innovation and key drivers of sustainable development. That includes ensuring access to affordable housing and reducing slum conditions. It also involves developing sustainable transportation systems (with an emphasis on mass transportation or low-carbon solutions). Investment in sustainable infrastructure and buildings is another priority and includes the development of sustainable water and lighting systems and construction processes.

As more and more people move to the cities, the protection and stewardship of suitable public spaces and parks will also be important. And, given that the majority of the world's cities are located on or near to the coast and rivers, the sustainable cities of the future must be able to protect citizens from climate change and water-related disasters.

How companies can help meet the goal

Sustainable city living is a particular strength for the corporate sector, especially those companies active in technology, construction and engineering. Siemens, Philips, Cisco, Google and IBM (to name but a few) are developing smart city products and strategies around lighting, heating logistics, traffic planning and even refuse collection. For example, in Barcelona, IBM has worked with the local government to develop a smarter way of organising refuge collection, while Philips has pioneered Lumimotion street lighting that relies on sensors to determine optimum lighting levels for the amount of street activity, hence providing a secure environment while saving energy.[16]

Goal 12. Responsible Consumption and Production

Goal 12 impacts every industry sector and puts a particular onus on the worlds of marketing and advertising. Our current levels of consumption are completely unsustainable. By 2050, we will need the equivalent of almost three planets to provide the natural resources needed to maintain current lifestyles. Our attitudes towards food pose a particular problem. An estimated one third of all food produced globally – worth about $1 trillion – is wasted either by consumers and retailers, or rots due to poor transportation and harvesting.[17]

The goal aims to implement a 10-year framework of programmes on sustainable consumption and production, with all countries taking action but developed countries taking the lead. A central target is, by 2030, to halve per capita global food waste at the retail and consumer levels as well as substantially reduce waste generation through prevention, reduction, recycling and reuse. Another key target is achieving the environmentally sound management of chemicals and all wastes throughout their life cycle, in accordance with agreed international frameworks. Also by 2030, people everywhere need to have the relevant information and awareness for sustainable development and lifestyles.

How companies can help meet the goal

Reducing consumer waste and promoting responsible consumption will require smarter products and services, better education and persuasive marketing. Over the past decade many food companies and retailers have committed to reducing food waste they create and to educate consumers about sustainable consumption – especially in areas like seafood and, increasingly, sugar and alcohol. Most major companies, meanwhile, have aggressive recycling targets not least because it makes good business sense to reduce costs. Hyundai, for example, targets an 85 percent recycling rate for the plastic, rubber and glass in its end-of-life vehicles, and a 95 percent recovery rate.[18]

In the consumer apparel sector, companies like Patagonia, Levi Strauss and Marks & Spencer have taken a leadership role in educating consumers about putting value on quality rather than quantity while even so-called fast fashion producers like H&M are starting to address the supply chain and sourcing problems linked to mass apparel manufacturing. Over the next 10 years the growth of sharing economy services, a Millennial emphasis on experience over material consumption and a societal move away from a cult of ownership could also have a big effect on consumption – but only if these new approaches also resonate in emerging economies.

Goal 13. Climate Action

Urgent action to combat climate change and minimise its disruptions is core to achieving the SDGs. The targets of Goal 13 include acknowledging the United Nations Framework Convention on Climate Change as the primary international, intergovernmental forum for negotiating the global response to climate change and improving education and awareness about climate change. Another target is for the private and public sector to jointly raise $100 billion annually by 2020 to address the climate needs of developing countries and fully mobilise the Green Climate Fund, a mechanism within the Framework Convention created to assist developing countries in adaptation and mitigation practices.

How companies can help meet the goals

The impacts of climate change are already hitting the supply chains and sourcing strategies of the world's major companies. In 2017 25 US corporations including Apple, Intel, Johnson Controls, Levi Strauss, Microsoft and VF Corporation took out full-page ads in *The New York Times*, *Wall Street Journal* and *New York Post* urging President Donald Trump to maintain the United States' commitments to the Paris climate accord. In terms of financial action, Swiss Re says that, by 2020, it will have advised 50 sovereign and sub-sovereign funds on climate risk resilience, and offered them $10 billion capacity against this risk.[19]

Goal 14. Life Below Water

More than 3 billion people depend on the world's oceans for their livelihoods and nearly 40 percent of the global population live in coastal communities. Oceans also help regulate the global ecosystem by absorbing heat and carbon dioxide from the atmosphere and protecting coastal areas from flooding and erosion. Altogether, the ocean-related economy is worth $28 trillion each year.[20] Yet this most precious resource faces grave threats from pollution, climate change, overfishing and consumer waste (notably plastic).

Goal 14 aims to prevent and significantly reduce marine pollution of all kinds, in particular from land-based sources including agriculture and consumer waste. It also seeks to minimise the impacts of ocean acidification, and effectively regulate harvesting and end overfishing. Another target focus on bringing economic benefits for vulnerable Small Island Developing States and developing countries through the sustainable use of fisheries, aquaculture and tourism.

How companies can help meet the goal

Obviously, the food and fishing industries have a direct responsibility for our oceans and so should be adhering to sustainable fishing practices. Many of the major grocers now adhere to the Marine Stewardship Council's guidance on sustainable sourcing of fish and seafood. In addition, industries that generate substantial chemical runoff and other ocean pollution have a responsibility that they may not have acknowledged in the past. The same is true for all companies that sell plastic products (and the consumers that discard them).

Carpet tile manufacturer, Interface, for example, upcycles discarded fishing nets into its products and Adidas has developed a new sneaker made from ocean trash. Smaller companies are equally innovative. Bureo turns recycled fishing nets from Chile into skateboard decks.

Goal 15. Life on Land

As with Goal 14 (Life Below Water), Goal 15 is also crucial for society and the planet. Central to preserving biodiversity and sustainable life for all is our stewardship of the world's forests, which cover 30 percent of the Earth's surface, help combat climate change, sustain some 1.6 billion people (including 70 million indigenous people), and are home to more than 80 percent of all terrestrial species of animals, plants and insects.[21]

In addition to the fragility of the world's forests our access to arable land also is under threat. More than half of the land used for agriculture is moderately or severely affected by soil degradation (much from industrial farming) with drought and desertification destroying 12 million hectares each year.[22]

Goal 15 aims, by 2020, to ensure the conservation, restoration and sustainable use of terrestrial and inland freshwater ecosystems, with a particular focus on forests, wetlands, mountains and drylands. It also promotes the implementation of sustainable management of all types of forests in order to halt deforestation.

By 2030 the goal aims to fully combat desertification and restore degraded land and soil while also conserving mountain ecosystems. Preserving biodiversity and protecting threatened species is another central theme.

How companies can help meet the goal

Multinational food companies such as Unilever, Cargill, Arla and Diageo have long collaborated through organisations like the Sustainable Agriculture Initiative Platform to create more sustainable approaches to agriculture and farming – but so much more needs to be done to combat global soil erosion and deforestation.[23] Likewise some of world's consumer goods companies are now leading on sustainable sourcing standards for palm oil after decades of widespread deforestation across Indonesia and Malaysia.[24] As described in Chapter 8, new food innovation around plant proteins so that the world can reduce its dependence on meat – especially beef – will play an important role in realising the goal. Technology will also continue to be important in monitoring and preventing illegal logging and trafficking of endangered species, while marketing also can help change people's perceptions about the type of food they consider desirable.

Goal 16. Peace, Justice and Strong Institutions

Goal 16 aims to tackle violence, corruption and exploitation throughout the world as peace and justice, and effective, accountable and inclusive institutions, are the social foundations that enable sustainable development. The main targets include significantly reducing all forms of violence and death rates;[25] ending all forms of violence and abuse towards children; promoting the rule of law; cutting down on arms trafficking and organised crime; and fighting bribery and establishing transparent institutions and good governance.

How companies help meet the goals

All companies have a responsibility for good governance and to combat corruption. Since 2012, Airbnb has created a standalone part of its platform to help refugees find safe, welcoming places to stay while they rebuild their lives after natural disasters, wars, conflict and other events. This platform was developed with some of the world's leading relief agencies who respond to global humanitarian crises as a tool for them to find housing for their communities quickly and easily.

Goal 17. Partnerships for the Goals

Strong collaboration, infrastructure and technological capacity are needed to execute and implement the other goals, especially in emerging nations. That's why Goal 17 aims to harness the combined power of governments, civil society, the private sector and the United Nations system. Despite the very active role that companies play within consumer societies around the world, they haven't been particularly active in supporting previous UN goals.

The targets of Goal 17 call for the business world to be more proactive in a number of ways including mobilising financial resources for developing countries; helping with debt support and relief; supporting developing countries as they build tax and other revenue collection systems; and providing environmentally sound technologies, particularly in the field of communication, at a cost level that developing economies can embrace.

How companies can help meet the goals

Getting the business world to work together and with external organisations to support the goals is a particular challenge but progress is being made. The World Business Council for Sustainable Development has gathered together 165 companies to work with 70 technology partners to accelerate the development of low-carbon technology solutions to stay below the 2°C climate change threshold.[26]

Q&A with David Croft, head of sustainability for Diageo

Q: What are the main sustainability issues your sector faces?

A: We identified the most material issues for our business and have developed clear targets for 2020 across three main areas. These targets align closely to the United Nations' SDGs.

First, it's critical for us that we enable people to enjoy alcohol responsibly and avoid misuse. We share the goal of the World Health Organisation: to reduce harmful use of alcohol by 10 percent by 2025. And we support more than 370 responsible drinking programmes in more than 40 countries – programmes that we know are making a difference.

Second, we aim to create shared value, enabling communities to develop and thrive, with basic resources and through empowerment and skills. This can be through our supply networks, with small farmers, or communities where we work, supporting gender empowerment and creating entrepreneurs that develop themselves and their communities.

Our third area of focus is to minimise our environmental impact. Reducing the water we use and replenishing water is essential for the future, while we are reducing our absolute carbon footprint through renewable energy options.

Q: Which issues do you think the public care about?

A: We know they increasingly care about all of these issues, from climate change to balanced lifestyles, and from human rights to sustainable agriculture. We focus on the issues that matter most within our business and where we can make greatest impact.

Q: How has a new type of always-connected consumer changed how Diageo's brands communicate around sustainability? Has the growth of social media expanded sustainability from a corporate stakeholder conversation to a brand marketing conversation?

A: Increasingly we see consumers wanting to know how we work, how we source the ingredients for our products and how we operate as a business. Their focus is on consumer brands as well as our corporate brand, and they are more connected than ever through social media. We focus on delivering both as a corporate stakeholder and through our brands, through how we work and how we collaborate with others. For example, on diversity and empowerment, our internal approach has led us to be a leader in female representation at senior leadership, while our PlanW programme has reached over 1.2 million people to support gender empowerment. Lastly our Smirnoff brand champions an inclusive society with a specific focus on gender as seen in its innovative DiscWoman campaign that highlights and tackles gender inequality in the electronic music scene.

Q: How is Diageo innovating to stay relevant for a changing, socially connected consumer?

A: We are constantly innovating, with new products and new techniques reaching consumers, in our communications and how we work. We look to leverage digital platforms to reach consumers and promote issues around our sustainability agenda and brands. The Johnnie Walker team has done some great work to reach consumers in this way, highlighting strength of character to promote change in its work in Colombia and around refugees coming to Europe alongside the NGO MercyCorp.

Q: What sustainability work being undertaken by Diageo you are most proud of?

A: Our work on water and diversity. Both connect across each of the levers we can use: how we work internally and within our supply networks, how we act as a corporate citizen and advocate for change, and how we connect to consumers to strengthen awareness in ways that motivates change. Our Water Blueprint describes our work to reduce water use in our production sites and the replenishment work we do, as well as outlining our commitment to deliver water, sanitation and hygiene (WASH) in the communities where we work within a wider water catchment area approach while also advocating for policy and wider support. The global partnership we have with WaterAid helps us delivery against these areas too, and we've found that our collective impact and voice is enhanced through working together. Similarly our diversity work internally, our PlanW programme, and our consumer facing work with Smirnoff is enhanced through our work with CARE International, with whom we initially collaborated to tackle the challenging issue of exploitation and harassment of women working in the hospitality sector in Cambodia and SE Asia. I expect both partnerships to grow from strength to strength, with greater impact as a result.

Q: Is there a Diageo sustainability campaign that you would highlight as epitomising the work the company wants to do, and why?

A: Our farming activity with smallholder farmers in sub-Saharan Africa is a great example of creating shared value. Through programmes that enable access to finance, better seeds and inputs, and even mechanisation and insurance, we are able to help smallholders with three or four acres to improve their productivity, sometimes up to 200 percent. This increases their livelihoods while also supporting a robust supply network for our local businesses that then don't need to use imports. This resulted in hundreds of millions being invested locally to benefit the wider economy alongside the smallholders themselves. One lady told me how the extra income meant she could keep her four children in school, and meant they have much greater chances going forward, while at the same time her increased farm yield supported better food security. This type of shared value delivers the aims we have and strive for.

Q: Many other industry sectors are coming to terms with sustainability disruption that will see less of their products consumed in the future.

Is your industry facing a similar challenge and, if so, how is it (and how is Diageo) responding?

A: We see the role of alcohol in society as a critical issue, and are constantly active in developing programmes that promote the avoidance of misuse of alcohol. These now include a global partnership with the United Nations in its IUITAR programme on road safety to avoid drink driving. Last year we had almost 350 programmes in different countries that help prevent misuse and we will continue to develop these individually and in partnership with other members of our industry.

Notes

1 www.oecd.org/dev/development-posts-how-will-the-world-raise.htm
2 www.huffingtonpost.co.uk/john-sauven/ocean-plastic-pollution_b_17484642.html
3 www.theguardian.com/visa-partner-zone/2015/jun/11/world-bank-group-unbanked-women-global-findex
4 http://www.foodaidfoundation.org/world-hunger-statistics.html
5 https://www.nutraingredients.com/Article/2016/06/13/Unilever-researchers-up-stock-cube-iron-bioavailability-using-food-additive
6 https://www.unglobalcompact.org/docs/issues_doc/development/SDGMatrix-ConsumerGoods.pdf
7 https://www.novartis.com/our-company/corporate-responsibility/expanding-access-healthcare/novartis-social-business/novartis-access
8 http://www.ab-inbev.com/better-world/a-healthier-world/global-smart-drinking-goals.html
9 https://www.unicef.org/publicpartnerships/files/EducationTheCaseForSupport.pdf
10 https://www.unilever.com/Images/uslp-unilever-sustainable-living-plan-scaling-for-impact-summary-of-progress-2014_tcm244-481642_en.pdf
11 https://sustainabledevelopment.un.org/sdg7
12 https://www.unglobalcompact.org/docs/issues_doc/development/SDGMatrix-Manufacturing.pdf
13 https://sustainabledevelopment.un.org/sdg9
14 https://www.unglobalcompact.org/docs/issues_doc/development/SDGMatrix-Manufacturing.pdf
15 https://www.gm.com/company/diversity/employee-resource-groups.html
16 www.youtube.com/watch?v=2S7W-DwC_-0
17 http://www.unric.org/en/food-waste/27133-one-third-of-all-food-wasted
18 https://www.unglobalcompact.org/docs/issues_doc/development/SDGMatrix_Transportation.pdf
19 https://www.unglobalcompact.org/docs/issues_doc/development/SDGMatrix_FinancialSvcs.pdf
20 https://sustainabledevelopment.un.org/sdg14
21 https://sustainabledevelopment.un.org/sdg15
22 Ibid.
23 www.saiplatform.org/
24 http://palmoilscorecard.panda.org/
25 https://sustainabledevelopment.un.org/sdg16
26 http://lctpi.wbcsd.org/

Epilogue

The temptation for many companies, as they contemplate how to meet major challenges like climate change, dwindling natural resources, and a global economy being ripped up and reshaped by technology, is to worry about these headaches later while focusing on the more pressing concerns of placating investor through quarterly profits now.

If that's how your business operates, then let me share a snapshot of how the world looks on August 6, 2017 as I conclude writing this book by glancing at a few headlines of the past few days.

- A dangerous heatwave, nicknamed Lucifer, is putting lives at risk throughout southern Europe, part of increasing climate change that could kill more than 150,000 people a year in the Mediterranean by the end of the century, Sky News reports.[1]
- A new report from Chatham House outlines how vulnerable global food supplies are to climate change, crumbling infrastructure and political unrest. It calls for global cooperation to prevent a crisis, writes the *Washington Post*.[2]
- The automobile industry is undergoing its greatest upheaval since its inception as European nations take concrete steps to phase out petrol-powered cars while new players like Lyft are entering the self-driving car market, the *Guardian* reports.[3]
- Fake news spread through social media is manipulating voters and stoking fears of mass bloodshed in Kenya's presidential elections, *The New York Times* reports. As with the UK Brexit vote and the United States and French presidential elections political trust is being eroded by secret and subversive forces.[4]

Those are just a few of the headlines of the past few days, but the themes of 21st century disruption repeat each week. Everywhere we look our world is being roiled on a political, financial, technological and environmental level.

These challenges are coming hard and fast and they are only going to continue. This then is the landscape all of society must navigate in the coming years. Governments, naturally, will be judged by how they act to protect and help society, but so will the corporate world – such is the influence and power that the companies of today wield. Those that show leadership to create a better world and society will thrive because they be providing the products and services consumers will need for a sustainable future. Those that don't? They will fail and very few people will miss them.

This book has tried to cover many of the sustainability areas where companies must succeed and communicate that success to win the public's trust. But if I were to try and distil its main themes I'd offer these takeaways to help plan for becoming a sustainable company and communicating why it is important.

1 Know what you stand for in today's changing world and make sure your employees understand and buy into it. Without their faith you will fail.
2 If you haven't worked out what you stand for yet, it's not too late to identify and develop your company's purpose. But remember that it has to represent how your entire business thinks and operates – not just how the marketing department would like to present you.
3 Some brands serve no sustainable purpose and don't deserve to exist (and no, delivering returns to shareholders isn't enough). The coming years will find them out.
4 No company is 100 percent sustainable. Every company has problems. But you will get credit for fixing what is wrong.
5 Trust is an elusive and moving target – you always have to keep earning it.
6 Give up trying to second guess the next generation from afar. Embrace and empower smart young people who already grasp the future.
7 If you've got something to hide, admit to the problem and solve it with transparency. In today's technology-enabled society, you will be found out.
8 Be honest about the future and prepare your employees and society for what you see. An honest discussion with consumers will help create demand for more sustainable products and help your business succeed.
9 Don't be afraid to lead in areas where your company has the expertise and experience to do so. Consumers want to trust the companies they buy from and will be open to your expertise if they believe you are genuine.
10 Admit what you don't know and collaborate with those who understand the new sustainable business landscape even if they are your competitors and critics. Only by working together can we reshape the various systems that business and society depends on for a sustainable future.

Finally, I'd like to reiterate one central thought. Having worked with companies on sustainability and having covered the growth of social media for the past decade, it is clear to me that most businesses and consumers have similar aspirations when it comes to shaping a more sustainable world. Yet, while some consumers will take an activist approach, most will be passive and wait for government and business to take the lead. Between government and business there is no contest: the corporate world is best prepared and motivated to drive sustainable change. So, if you work in business, what are you waiting for? There's no time to waste.

Notes

1 http://news.sky.com/story/heatwaves-in-europe-may-kill-150000-each-year-10974670
2 www.washingtonpost.com/news/wonk/wp/2017/07/27/how-the-climate-crisis-could-become-a-food-crisis-overnight/?utm_term=.36bf76517378
3 https://www.theguardian.com/commentisfree/2017/jul/26/cars-eu-tories-diesel-petrol-vans-european-environment
4 https://www.nytimes.com/2017/08/06/world/africa/kenya-election-kenyatta-odinga.html?_r=0

Selected bibliography

Belz, Frank-Martin and Peattie, Ken (2012). *Sustainability Marketing*: Wiley

Bhattacharya, C.B., Sen, Sankar and Korschun, Daniel (2011). *Leveraging Corporate Responsibility*: Cambridge University Press

Caradonna, Jeremy L. (2014). *Sustainability: A History*: Oxford University Press

Friedman, Thomas (2016). *Thank You for Being Late*: Allen Lane

Gillmor, Dan (2006). *We the Media*: O'Reilly

Levine, Rick, Locke, Christopher, Searls, Doc and Weinberger, David (2007). *The Cluetrain Manifesto*: Basic Books

Li, Charlene and Bernoff, Josh (2011). *Groundswell*: Harvard Business Press

Lury, Celia (2010). *Consumer Culture*: Polity Books

Pollan, Michael (2007). *The Omnivore's Dilemma*

Rheingold, Howard (2003). *Smart Mobs: The Next Social Revolution*: Basic Books

Ross, Alec (2016). *The Industries of the Future*: Simon & Schuster

Schlosser, Eric (2012). *Fast Food Nation*: Houghton Mifflin

Serrin, Judith and Serrin, William (eds.) (2002). *Muckraking: The Journalism that Changed America*: The New Press

Sheldrake, Philip (2011). *The Business of Influence*: Wiley

Streitmatter, Rodger (2011). *Mightier than the Sword: How the News Media Have Shaped American History*: Westview

Tapscott, Don and Ticoll, David (2012). *The Naked Corporation*: Free Press

Tungate, Mark (2013). *Adland*: Kogan Page

Wallman, James (2014). *Stuffocation*: Penguin

Warner, Bernhard and Yeomans, Matthew (2012). *#FAIL: The 50 Greatest Social Media Screw-Ups*: SMI Publishing

Wollen, Peter and Kerr, Joe (2002) *Autopia: Cars and Culture*: Reaktion Books

Wu, Tim (2017). *The Attention Merchants*: Atlantic Books

Index